A VOICE WAS SOUNDING

SELECTIONS FROM *THIS LAND*

VOL
4

**THIS LAND
PRESS**

Copyright © 2014 by This Land Press

All rights reserved, including right of reproduction
in whole or part in any form.

Works appearing in this anthology were originally
published between January and December 2013 in
This Land, Tulsa, OK.

Vincent LoVoi, Publisher; Michael Mason, Editor

WWW.THISLANDPRESS.COM

Book designed by This Land Press.
Printed in the United States of America.

First Edition, November 2014

ISBN: 978-0-9858487-8-1

PRAISE FOR *THIS LAND*

"A rare example of literary journalism... *The New Yorker* with balls."

—*Columbia Journalism Review*

"I first discovered This Land Press in 2012, and I am so glad that I did. In just a short time, they have created something special not just for readers in Tulsa, but for the rest of us around the world. With outstanding storytelling, thoughtful reporting, and truly diverse voices, they've become a model for the future of journalism with a real sense of place."

— Mark Armstrong, *Longreads*

"*This Land* suggests the kind of pioneering spirit that Woody Guthrie would likely approve."

—*Monocle* magazine

"Nobody tells our story like *This Land*. In this eclectic and compulsively readable volume, essays of character and place, portrait and memoir, tightly researched journalism, and delectable fiction all combine to create a whole that is much larger than its parts. *A Voice Was Sounding* is a tapestry, a feast, a tamed cacophony that evokes not merely the heartland of America but its very heart: bitter, self-obsessed, self-deprecating, glorious. Here is a collection of writings from the center of America that is as disparate and wild and strange as the land from which it springs."

— Rilla Askew, *Fire in Beulah*

"I love this!"

—David Carr, *The New York Times*

"A tapestry, a feast, a tamed cacophony that evokes not merely the heartland of America but its very heart."
—Rilla Askew, *Fire in Beulah*

A VOICE WAS SOUNDING

SELECTIONS FROM
THIS LAND

VOL
4

Compelling journalism
and heartfelt stories from
the middle of America

EDITED BY
**Michael Mason
& Natasha Ball**

CONTENTS

Introduction
by Natasha Ball · **v**

From One Fire
by Marcos Barbery · **1**

Youngwolfe Accused
by Hunter Howe Cates · **35**

Watts and Clary
by Steve Gerkin · **43**

Terror's Legacy
by Jason Christian · **51**

Dogs Playing Poker
by Brian Ted Jones · **59**

Home on the Range
by Natasha Ball · **67**

Locker Room Confidential
by Russell Cobb · **73**

Horses and Dagger
by Jennie Lloyd · **81**

Snakes on a Plain
by Holly Wall · **95**

Petro State
by James McGirk · **105**

Subterranean Psychonaut
by Michael Mason, Chris Sandel, and Lee Roy Chapman · **115**

Weird Al-Chemy
by Mitch Gilliam · **153**

Pop Life
by Steve Sherman · **159**

Borrowed Notes
by Cortney Stone · **165**

Searching for John Joseph Mathews
by Richard Higgs · **171**

A Symphony of Bees
by Mark Brown · **181**

A Stiller Ground
by Gordon Grice · **197**

A
VOICE
WAS
SOUNDING

SELECTIONS FROM *THIS LAND*

VOL

4

INTRODUCTION

By *Natasha Ball*

I DROVE TO MY OFFICE AT THIS LAND PRESS through the lingering smoke of bottle rockets on the weekend of Fourth of July 2013. That same weekend a decade ago, a gruesome, mind-bending scene unfolded: five lives converged on the 14th floor of Tulsa's downtown DoubleTree Hotel for a few days of sex, drugs, and other fireworks. After an imploded love triangle and a bathtub torture session, a monster story was born, yet remained largely untold. After mentions fell out of the papers, the story of local prep school graduate Gordon Todd Skinner lingered on as legend in Tulsa.

Two years prior, I was a journalist-turned-blogger who wrote about concerts and kids' activities for websites read by working mothers and other weekend warriors—not exactly anyone's first choice for a staffer at a journalism start-up that, in just its first few issues, had charged head-on into Tulsa's problem with corrupt cops, offered an account of growing up gay in the family headed by the granddaddy of all televangelists, and revealed the dark history of the city's most exciting entertainment district.

This Land was founded as an effort to build the literature of our community, to see what we could grow by applying journalism and storytelling across various media to neighborhood lore. If that formu-

vii

la was the hunch, then the Skinner saga was the treasure map. Hours of late-night and early-morning conversations around the office pointed to the urgency we felt to make sense of the pull of this place. All roads, if followed to the dirt, led to Oklahoma, it seemed. Problem was, these stories had either been lost or, due to the limited resources, inattention, and, in some cases, arrogance of the established media here, not given their due. These stories had sunk into the substrate. There was deep digging that needed doing, and the ones who gathered to create *This Land* had long dispensed with spades.

With the Skinner story, which we called "Subterranean Psychonaut," Tulsa asserted and reasserted itself as a character, like a clandestine agent smirking from the background of one too many famous photos. That Saturday, contributors Chris Sandel and Lee Roy Chapman, editor Michael Mason, and I built the first few drafts of what would become the most well-read story in *This Land's* history. It was also our heftiest, a labyrinth of global proportions starring a host of recognizable locals and an alphabet soup of federal agencies, cooked down to an economical 13,000 words. Online, the text is augmented by galleries of never-before-published photos, audio recordings, source documents, and other rabbit holes, the kind that marry good journalism with experience—a virtual day trip, as it were. It glowed on the faces of readers from Tulsa to Australia; we found shaggy copies of the story in print on armchairs and magazine racks around town, well thumbed by a community not on anyone's list of reading cities.

That weekend wasn't the only one spent with Skinner. The writing and editing, design and art gathering, checking and double-checking—not an unusual dance, one we did at *This Land* as part of stories great and small, but one that, as a journalist minted in an era when print was dead and something the media bosses called content was king, felt decadent, like a revolt. Meanwhile, we kept a few other plates spinning. We published a twice-monthly magazine, each created as an episode on its own as well as the latest installment of a running conversation about the meaning of life and culture in Oklahoma. The design, created in the same spirit as the stories inside, turned each issue into an eagerly anticipated collector's item. Our readers began to send us photos from their mailboxes on new-issue day.

INTRODUCTION

That same season, we planned the release of a feature film, one that documented the unknown history of Native American hymn as the heart of America's original music traditions. We compiled and published books of memoir, nonfiction, travel, and poetry. We built a store and stocked it with t-shirts stamped with our frying-pan shaped state; a few we saved for ourselves, wearing them everywhere t-shirts were allowed, signing on as walking advertisements for a for-profit, new-media venture in a place that hadn't seen such a thing since the dailies laid off the last newsboys. Too, we brought together one of the largest online communities in the state, with a population to beat that of most towns we visited.

Somewhere in between, we baked cakes for each other's birthdays and threw pot-luck dinners on the office front lawn. Rarely did we pass up a chance to pay tribute to how we, a motley crew of journalists, writers, and artists from all over as well as around here, could wander in and out of each other's offices to borrow notebooks, microphones, and, occasionally, a talisman for good luck. By then it had been a couple of years since Michael Mason, our founder and editor, pitched me the idea of This Land Press, which he then envisioned as a co-op of media makers. By the time I saw him again, then with Vince LoVoi and a round of the ramen dish that helped seal so many deals in those early days, he and a group of some of the most talented and celebrated storytellers in the country had launched a company that had Tulsa abuzz and had turned the heads of America's top media critics. Their invitation to join the staff and work full-time on stories centered on the place that, as a fifth-generation Oklahoman, might actually run in my veins, was less a proposal than a dare. They had the proof that stories change things. The people and places that slip by us every day get fixed in the sky. It makes it easier to tell where we are and where to go next. What I couldn't resist was the opportunity to drive abandoned streets on holiday weekends, to join the trees in knowing what lies beneath.

This volume of *A Voice Was Sounding* represents the spoils of many a good dig. The writers cut deals with snake caves and suburban bee hives, with the capital of the state's largest Indian nation and a specter in the Osage Hills, not to mention a log cabin in a pine forest

ix

NATASHA BALL

and the 100-year-old dust that drew Steinbeck. In exchange they got their monsters and heroes, finding them, as they are when one digs deep under the quiet boulevards, one and the same. As it was with so many projects, and "Subterranean Psychonaut" was certainly one, everyone in the office, from the film and audio crews to design, distribution, and the collaborators at large, could point to the spots where they left fingerprints. My joy is knowing where to look to see them overlap, proof of the kind of work that leaves the earth upturned.

Natasha Ball was This Land's *managing editor in 2013.*

FROM ONE FIRE

An epic struggle between the Cherokee Nation and its
Freedman for Native rights.

By *Marcos Barbery*

ON AN OPPRESSIVELY HOT EVENING LAST MAY, David Cornsilk
addressed a room of so-called "black Indians" at Gilcrease Hills Baptist
Church in northwest Tulsa. He wore a leather-braided bolo tie clasped
by an emerald quartz. Though Cornsilk never formally studied law, his
voice bellowed with the rhetorical ire of a white-shoed seasoned litigator.

"By a show of hands, how many folks here tonight are Freedmen?"
Cornsilk asked into the microphone. Each raised an arm. Visibly dismayed,
Cornsilk shook his head. It was a trick question.

"No," Cornsilk said. "The Freedmen died a long time ago. You are
not Freedmen. You are Cherokee, and it is time that you begin to recognize who you are."

Cornsilk is Cherokee, and a self-taught civil rights advocate and
genealogist. He traces his slave-owning ancestors back to their aboriginal lands of Georgia and Tennessee—to a period before the Trail of
Tears. Cornsilk is not a Cherokee Freedmen descendant. For nearly two
decades, however, Cornsilk fought for the citizenship rights of Freedmen
descendants—blacks who descend from slaves once owned by Cherokee
and other tribes.

While working full-time as a clerk at Petsmart, Cornsilk took on America's second-largest Indian tribe, the Cherokee Nation, in what led to a landmark tribal decision. Cornsilk served as a lay advocate, which permits non-lawyers to try cases before the Cherokee Nation's highest court. When Cornsilk was not unloading dog food from truck beds and stocking shelves under the sounds of chirping parakeets, he composed legal briefs on the rights of Freedmen descendants, made oral arguments in court, and responded to a flurry of technical motions submitted by his opponents.

The legal advocacy would come at a personal cost for Cornsilk. Not long after his talk at Gilcrease Hills, he was unable to maintain two full-time jobs. So he sacrificed one. No sooner, Cornsilk failed to make rent on his one-bedroom apartment in Tulsa. He broke the lease and moved into his Honda Civic while seeking new employment. He began showering at the YMCA.

Outmatched and outspent by a team of Cherokee Nation lawyers, few considered Cornsilk a threat, and certainly not someone who could ignite debate on race and tribal power—but he did, and that debate would end up costing the Cherokee Nation millions of dollars in attorney's fees, lobbyists, and public relations campaigns.

The ongoing battle for tribal equal rights for Freedmen descendants has grown increasingly urgent. With other American Indian tribes across Oklahoma closely watching the impending U.S. court cases to signal the fate of their own Freedmen descendants and the extent of their sovereignty, Cornsilk believes that the present stakes could not be higher.

Not surprisingly, Cornsilk has grown more polemical. At the Baptist church Cornsilk said that if you do not think these folks in this room "have Cherokee ancestry and you have not done the research to find out, then you're a racist." Part of what helps make him so compelling is that on the surface—like Cherokee Principal Chief Bill John Baker and members of the Cherokee Nation Tribal Council—Cornsilk looks white.

OPPRESSED BY THE OPPRESSED

Headquartered in Tahlequah, Oklahoma, the Cherokee Nation and its wholly owned business arm earned over a billion dollars last year through a myriad of businesses such as gaming, U.S. Department of

Defense contracts, and federally funded programs. Today, taxpayers help support the Cherokee Nation through federal grants.

The brutality committed by whites against American Indians—especially the Trail of Tears—has become a part of our national conscience. Yet it is hard to imagine that during this period an even more poorly documented atrocity was being perpetrated: The Cherokee were slave owners long before their forced removal from the southern states.

By the time gold was discovered in Georgia at the dawn of the 19th century, Cherokee slave codes were indistinguishable from those enacted by the rest of the South. Soon after, when the U.S. Indian Removal Act forced Cherokee and other Indians to relinquish their native land and move west, countless blacks enslaved by Cherokees crossed into the frontier bound and shackled. These black slaves suffered a far more violent experience than their Indian masters.

Nearly a third of the Cherokee Nation's citizens lost their lives during the Trail of Tears; the number of their slaves killed remains unknown. Once the Cherokee Nation arrived in what later became Oklahoma, they prospered in part due to their agrarian roots, large-scale plantations, and practice of slavery.

Three decades later, when the Lincoln administration threatened slaveholders, the Cherokee Nation signed allegiance with the Confederacy. Finding themselves on the losing side of the Civil War, and their shrinking territory under threat once again, the Cherokee Nation sought to re-establish government-to-government relations with the US.

In the summer of 1866, just months after U.S. lawmakers amended the Constitution to bar slavery, the Cherokee Nation entered into a treaty with the federal government. Among a long list of terms, the treaty granted perpetual freedom and full tribal membership to Cherokee slaves and their descendants. The Treaty of 1866 named these black, newly minted Cherokee members "Freedmen."

FREEDMEN AND TRIBAL BENEFITS

From the last row of Gilcrease Hills Baptist Church's recreation hall, Kenneth Payton listened to David Cornsilk's voice rise and fall. Payton looks like a professional basketball player. He is six foot five, wears a tracksuit, and drives a pick-up. Payton lives in Broken Arrow with his wife and three of his four boys. His young sons append the word "sir" to their responses, hinting at their father's service in the United States Army. When we first met, Payton's hand enveloped mine.

Payton and other Freedmen descendants are represented in the pending U.S. court case by Jon Velie, who is a licensed attorney based in Norman. Velie describes Payton as a "Cherokee of African descent." The unfolding lawsuit led by Velie challenges the Cherokee Nation's dismissal of its former black citizens. "It's not a damages case," Velie said. "The Freedmen citizens simply want to be reinstated as full members of the tribe."

The ongoing litigation demands that the federal government enforce the 147-year-old treaty between the United States and Cherokee Nation, and restore tribal citizenship to Payton, his children, and potentially, tens of thousands of others who share similar ancestry. "I tell my kids all the time, 'You are Cherokee,' " Payton said. "And they say, 'Oh Dad, he is crazy,' but it is true. We are Cherokee."

Payton is not alone. During the year I spent reporting this story, nearly everyone I met in Oklahoma claimed Indian heritage. To many, the notion that Indian blood pumps through them, irrespective of quantum or degree, is a birthright. It suggests a dual identity. And it insinuates indigenous roots—a deeper, more authentic tie to land and country that predates statehood and union. But unlike most, Payton possesses the documents to back his claims.

After a rare public debate between Jon Velie and the Cherokee Nation's Attorney General Todd Hembree, a young man stood to ask a question. Until this moment, the debate on Freedmen held at the University of Oklahoma School of Law had been pointed, though relatively cordial. An event organizer rushed to furnish the young Indian a wireless microphone. "What I do not understand is, what is it that these people want?" the young man demanded, directing his questions about the Freedmen at Velie. His voice did not require amplification. "What do they actually want? Or as my parents and grandparents would say, *Gado usdi unaduli?*"

I later learned that the young man's name is Corey Still. He was a senior at the University of Oklahoma, and a full-blood Cherokee. Addressing Velie and the audience in his native Cherokee tongue was laced in subtext. If anyone else in the auditorium spoke Cherokee, including

Freedmen descendants, it was not apparent. Cherokee Nation Attorney General Hembree has long argued that because his tribe is an independent sovereign with a distinct culture, it has an absolute right to self-determine its criteria for citizenship. Corey Still struck at the heart of a different, more veiled, but no less present sentiment.

To Payton and other Freedmen descendants, their ongoing lawsuit is about acceptance. Payton seeks on behalf of his family, living and dead, recognition of his tribal identity. But implicit in the enforcement of a century-old treaty—and this is what Corey Still was alluding to—are the present-day benefits that come with tribal citizenship: free health care, educational scholarships, and housing assistance, to name a few. In Indian country, the idea that black "non-Indians" are unjustly suing tribes solely for economic benefits has been the source of much racially charged vitriol.

Several months after the debate, clutching his birth certificate and grandparents' death certificates, Payton drove his pick-up from Broken Arrow to Tahlequah. Dense woods conceal the Cherokee Heritage Center's genealogy center, which offers free services to would-be Cherokee. Gene Norris, the center's senior genealogist, told Payton that Cherokee citizenship is determined by linking an ancestor to the federal Dawes Rolls, which were completed in 1907. Norris inspected the authenticity of Payton's paperwork, led Payton to a computer, and searched for Payton's relatives on a digitized version of the rolls.

"Here's Emma," Norris said. Norris discovered Emma Mackee, Payton's great-grandmother, listed on the rolls. He then attempted to explain that there are subsections to the rolls. They include "By Blood" and "Freedmen," among others. The nuance left Payton scratching his shaved head. Your great-grandmother is on the Freedmen subsection, Norris explained, adding that until the litigation is resolved, the Cherokee Nation is not accepting any Freedmen applications for citizenship.

"You can go ahead and apply but they probably won't process it," Norris said.

INDIAN BLOOD

For hundreds of years, the question of who is an Indian has vexed the federal government and tribes alike. By the end of the 19th century, being an Indian usually came with one of two things: benefit or despair. More often, it came with both at once. Tribal economic benefits encouraged fraudulent citizenship claims by white, non-Indian imposters. Despair drove many true Indians away from federal officials.

Up until 1893, the dozens of tribes residing in Indian Territory owned millions of acres communally. The Cherokee Nation was the largest and most powerful tribe among them. Cloaked under efforts to assimilate Indians into American society and usher greater economic opportunity, in 1887, the federal government passed a law that began negotiations to chop up tribal lands. A federal commission was later organized and tasked with persuading the Cherokee Nation and other major tribes—known as the Five Civilized Tribes—to carve their land into allotments that could be bought and sold. The man appointed to lead the commission was a former abolitionist Massachusetts Senator named Henry Dawes.

On November 28, 1893, U.S. Secretary of the Interior Hoke Smith[1] issued instructions to Dawes and other commission members. The contents of that letter, according to Kent Carter, author of *The Dawes Commission and the Allotment of the Five Civilized Tribes*, were not made public at the time.

"Success in your negotiations will mean the total abolition of the tribal autonomy of the Five Civilized Tribes and the wiping out the quasi-independent governments within our territorial limits," Smith wrote to Dawes. The feds were making way for the 46th state: Oklahoma, which derives from Choctaw words, "okla" and "huma," or "red" and "people."

---

1. After U.S. Secretary of the Interior, Hoke Smith, wrote the letter to the Dawes Commission demanding the abolition of tribal governments, he moved from Washington, D.C., to Georgia. In 1906, Hoke Smith ran successfully for governor—an event that sparked race riots across Georgia's capital. Hoke Smith ran on a platform promising to pass a state constitutional amendment striping the voting rights of blacks. The Civil War had ended nearly half a century earlier, freeing slaves and outlawing its practice across the country. Yet under Hoke Smith's administration, Georgia passed some of the most virulent Jim Crow laws. Over the next six decades, they assured the dominance of white political and economic power at the expense of blacks.

FROM ONE FIRE

Tribes "absolutely decided to take a united front and oppose the allotment of their land and the termination of tribal governments," Dr. Brad Agnew, a history professor at Northeastern State University in Tahlequah, said. After multiple attempts, Dawes failed to convince leaders of the Cherokee Nation to split and relinquish their lands. Congress responded by passing another law. In 1898—just a year after the region's first commercial oil well was drilled[2]—a new federal law effectively forced the Cherokee Nation and other tribes into submission. The plan: Each Indian citizen or head of household would be granted over a hundred acres. Before the land could be divided, Dawes and his commission had to answer: Who is an Indian?

The challenge was further complicated by internal tribal factions, which were a consequence of removal. Over time, many white colonialists had married into the tribe, and their light-skinned descendants often ascended to positions of power. "If you look at pictures of the leaders of the Cherokee Nation, most of them, they dressed white, they looked white," Professor Agnew said. "They were white for all intents and purposes." Principal Chief John Ross, for instance, who led the Cherokee Nation from 1828 until his death in 1866, was seven-eighths Scottish.[3]

---

2. The Nellie Johnstone Number One was the first commercial oil well drilled in what was then Indian Territory. After obtaining a lease from the Cherokee Nation, George Keeler, William Johnstone, and Frank Overlees, working with the Cudahy Oil Company, drilled the well on April 15, 1897. According to Frank F. Finny, in *Chronicles of Oklahoma*, until the "Cudahy well came in the evidence that oil could be found in important quantities in Indian Territory was inconclusive... "

3. Subsections of the Dawes Rolls served to distinguish the tribe's primary factions: mixed-bloods, full-bloods, adopted Indians, and Freedmen. Historians argue that the distinctions were designed not because one group listed on the Dawes Rolls was considered more or less Indian than the other, but rather to protect the economic interests of full-bloods, who were still rooted in their own language and culture. Many full-bloods were so distrustful of the federal government that they hid out from Dawes commissioners. "The tragedy is, those who are the most Indian are not considered Indian today," Professor Agnew said. Many Freedmen, meanwhile, descended not just from slaves but African mothers and Cherokee fathers. "Masters frequently made use of female slaves, and those slaves produced children," Agnew explained. "John Ross was an eighth Indian. And I suspect that many of the Freedmen have more Indian blood than that."

7

While the Dawes Rolls were finalized, a succession of new oil wells sprouted across the region. Railroad systems linking east and west coasts that had once been obstructed by Indian reservations were either fully connected or on the way to becoming so. During his final years, Senator Dawes, who had once been viewed as a friend to American Indians, was plagued by sickness. He died in 1903. His colleagues helped finish what historians agree was a herculean task.

The federal Dawes Rolls of the Five Civilized Tribes closed on March 5, 1907, superseding all previous Indian citizenship rolls. Seven months later, tribal jurisdictions crumbled. Borders of what had been Oklahoma Territory were expanded and redrawn. Oklahoma became a state on November 16, 1907. At its birth, Oklahoma was the leading oil-producing state in U.S. It would maintain that distinction until 1921—the same year, it turns out, Oklahoma's Adair county would earn two distinctions of its own: highest concentration of Cherokee full-blood residents, and poorest county in the nation.

STATE OF THE NATION

During Labor Day weekend of 2012, as most Americans relished the final days of summer, the Cherokee Nation erupted in celebration. The festivities marked the commemoration of the signing of the Cherokee Tribal Constitution. On Friday night, a powwow commenced the weekend's events. Beads of sweat streamed down faces masked in paint. Full-blood Cherokees cloaked in tribal regalia—brightly colored feathered headdresses, leather leggings, and beaded dresses—howled and chanted and struck communal drums. Hundreds danced to the throbbing beats. Cherokee folklore says that the pounding of drums embody the tribe's pulsing heart and enduring fire.

For three days, over the course of dozens of dizzying events, despite a dogged heat, potent displays of tribal nationalism did not subside. "Once that fire dies down, then that's when all the tribes will die down," a young Cherokee said, "and it is our job to pass it from generation to generation." If the federal government had attempted to wipe out the Cherokee Nation, they had done so in vain. Bill John Baker, Principal Chief of the Cherokee Nation, who has a shock of white hair, spent the long weekend promoting a message of tribal unification. He seemed to

FROM ONE FIRE

emerge magically at each event, serving as master of ceremonies. "We all come from one fire," Chief Baker said.

To Rodslen Brown-King, a Freedmen descendant, Chief Baker's message stood in contrast to his actions—or lack there of—upon entering office. Cherokee people, she says, derive from "one fire," but it is the inclusion of the Freedmen in that metaphor where her interpretation diverges from the chief's. The morning after the powwow, Brown-King, her three brothers, eight sisters, two sons, two daughters, and ten grandchildren, displayed their own message of tribal unification—not in a courtroom but in the Cherokee Holiday Parade. Just after dawn on Saturday, Brown-King and her family applied final touches to their Freedmen parade float, which included an eight-foot working waterfall. Before the parade began, sidewalks lining Tahlequah's Muskogee Avenue were littered with lawn chairs and young families eager to secure good views.

Between floats, sirens wailed as local fireman crammed in buzzing go-carts spun in circles. A college marching band honked freshly polished golden horns. As the army of floats drifted down the street, it grew increasingly apparent that nearly everyone—both parade participants and bystanders packing the streets—looked the same: white. The full-blood Cherokee who had starred at the powwow the night before had all but vanished. Save for Rodslen Brown-King and her family, no other blacks were in sight. So when they were finally directed by tribal officials to pull their oversized pick-up truck into the parade line, it was not just the extravagance of their float that drew attention.

Rodslen, who is in her late 40s, fit, and has long, locked hair, jogged alongside the Freedmen float. She waved and tossed candies to the small children dotting the street. As the Freedmen float rolled by, an elderly white woman seated in a canvas chair rocked her head back and forth in apparent disgust. The overwhelming majority of those in attendance, however, cheered Rodslen and her family along. Most agreed that the Freedmen float was impressive. Willoman Brown, Jr., Rodslen's son, gazed at onlookers as he steered the pick-up pulling the float with one hand on the wheel and an elbow fixed on the window ledge. "They welcomed us. It was quite unusual," he said. "The way they looked at us and clapped, it was like, 'Glad y'all here. You made it.' "

9

Several hours after the parade, on the other side of town, Chief Baker delivered his State of the Nation address to a large, air-conditioned auditorium. More than once, he was overcome by emotion. While discussing his efforts to bridge a divided Cherokee Nation, Chief Baker choked up. He was forced to pause until the threat of his own tears subsided. U.S. Congressman Tom Cole and Baker's cabinet, including Attorney General Todd Hemebree, along with members of the Cherokee Nation Tribal Council, crowded the first rows. Baker's predecessor, Chief Chad Smith, who led the Cherokee Nation for 12 years—and oversaw a tribal constitutional amendment that removed Freedmen descendants—did not attend. During last year's highly contested tribal election, Smith lost to Baker by a sliver of votes.

Chief Baker did not mention the Freedmen descendants, or how their ongoing litigation bled into the election he ultimately won. Baker did not bring up or explain why, just a year earlier, the federal government turned off a faucet flowing millions of dollars to the Cherokee Nation. And he did not mention the costs—both to the Cherokee Nation's coffers and reputation—of maintaining the fight to keep Kenneth Payton, Rodslen Brown-King, and thousands more Freedmen descendants out of the tribe.

The exclusion of the Freedmen in Chief Baker's State of the Nation speech reflects the chasm between how the tribe perceives itself internally and how outsiders perceive it. For a tribe that has fallen victim to unspeakable crimes historically, it is difficult to accept its own original sin. "We never held slaves," an elderly full-blood Cherokee told me after the speech.[4] Perhaps the reason Chief Baker passed over the Freedmen is because so few members of the tribe acknowledge their own stained history, let alone recent events that shaped the Freedmen dissension. Advocates say that much of what occurred in the Freedmen case took place in secret, or as a tribal judge put it, "through silence."

---

4. Many Cherokee slaves were branded like cattle, stripped of their identity, and bestowed with the surnames of their Cherokee masters. According to Rudi Halliburton, Jr., author of *Red Over Black: Black Slavery Among the Cherokee Indians*, slaves who attempted to escape—and there were many—were hunted with dogs. Cherokee militias were often formed to track and capture runaway slaves, who were promptly returned to their masters or publicly executed, serving as a warning to others.

The 2007 constitutional amendment that permanently removed the Freedmen descendants, even Attorney General Hembree concedes, was done in haste. In that special election, which clenched the disenfranchisement of Freedmen descendants, less than seven percent of the tribe cast votes. The Freedmen descendants are easy to ignore. They make up a minority of the tribe. But like African Americans in state and national elections, Freedmen descendants might constitute a powerful block. After more than a century maintaining tribal voting rights, it was this threat—the fear that the Freedmen descendants may band together to unseat an incumbent chief—that first led to their ouster. The extent of their unwillingness to go quietly was impossible to foresee. So too was the resolve of their advocates.

THE RISE OF DAVID CORNSILK

The two men met while standing beside each other under a blistering sun. The line to vote for the next Cherokee Principal Chief snaked around the courthouse. The man who would later reach the voter registration table first was elderly, smallish, and appeared black. The man who stood directly behind him was young, tall, and appeared white. It was 1983—a century after the Dawes Commission was established. As the line inched forward, the two men struck up a conversation on tribal politics and Oklahoma's relentless heat. The black man introduced himself as Roger Nero. The white man introduced himself as David Cornsilk.

When Nero reached the registration table, a light-skinned Cherokee woman requested to see Nero's tribal identification card. " 'We don't let you people vote anymore,' " Cornsilk recalled the tribal official saying to Nero. The official instructed Nero to vacate the building. "When I handed her my card, she smiled and said no problem and handed me a ballot," Cornsilk said. Cornsilk did not discover until after the election that Nero was a Freedmen descendant. At the time, Nero was 82. He was an infant during Oklahoma statehood; Nero's name appears on the original Dawes Rolls.

Nero filed a lawsuit against the tribe in U.S. courts. The court dismissed the suit and ruled that Nero's case was a tribal matter. "He was old and didn't have any money and pretty much let it go," Cornsilk said. Nero's failure to gather traction and his subsequent death haunted Cornsilk, who later landed a position within the Cherokee Nation's department of tribal registration. "Part of my job was to deal with Freedmen applicants," Cornsilk said. "I started reading their histories, and I came to the realization that we really screwed these people."

During the two decades that followed, Cornsilk advocated for the rights of Freedmen descendants with mixed results. In 1988, while still a tribal employee, he wrote a letter of protest on behalf of Freedmen—garnering the support of six additional tribal employees who signed in solidarity—and sent it to then-Principal Chief Wilma Mankiller. Cornsilk told me that his letter resulted in threats by senior tribal officials. "I never heard from the chief, but I got a call from the chief's aide who said, 'We do not talk about the Freedmen, and anyone who does, does not work for the tribe.'" Tribal officials deny these claims.

After a decade of advocating for the Freedmen while still a tribal employee, Cornsilk grew disenchanted by tribal leadership. He quit working for the tribe, and after a quick stint working for the Bureau of Indian Affairs in Washington, D.C., Cornsilk returned to Tahlequah to begin his work as an official "lay advocate." After an elderly black woman named Bernice Riggs was denied Cherokee citizenship by the tribe, Cornsilk obtained permission from the Cherokee tribal court to petition an appeal on her behalf. Cornsilk said that Cherokee tribal members told him that Riggs lived on "Nigger Hill," a neighborhood outside Tahlequah where many Freedmen descendants reside. The Riggs case was not successful, yet it solidified Cornsilk as an unwavering Freedmen advocate.

With a receding hairline and newly separated from his full-blood Cherokee wife, Cornsilk moved to Tulsa in 2000 and accepted a full-time clerk position at Petsmart. While working there in the summer of 2003, Cornsilk received a phone call from Marilyn Vann, an engineer by trade, and leader of the Freedmen Descendants of the Five Civilized Tribes. Jon Velie, the Norman-based attorney, represents Vann.

FROM ONE FIRE

After helping to bring legal action against the Seminole Nation several years earlier, Velie earned a reputation as a civil rights attorney.[5] In 2000, the Seminole Nation, which is smaller than the Cherokee Nation and based in Wewoka, stripped their Freedmen descendants of citizenship rights with a tribal constitutional amendment. Velie was part of the legal team that secured a federal court decision in favor of Seminole Freedmen. Now, with Velie on the Cherokee Freedmen case pro bono, he and Vann were preparing a legal offensive against the Cherokee Nation.

Vann called Cornsilk and invited him to address a Freedmen descendants' meeting in north Tulsa. Vann believed that Cornsilk understood the Freedmen plight as well as anyone. "He knew a great deal about Cherokee law and history and genealogy," Vann said.

To Vann and other Freedmen advocates, the summer of 2003 brought with it a great sense of urgency. Principal Chief Chad Smith, who was first elected to the tribe's highest office in 1999, had just clinched his second term. According to Cornsilk, designating Cherokee Freedmen as "non-Indians" was a priority throughout Smith's first term. That May, Cherokee Freedmen descendants were excluded from the general election that secured Smith's second term.

But there was something else at stake during the 2003 general tribal election to which the Freedmen were not a party. Smith had run in part on a platform to remove federal oversight of the Cherokee Nation. At the time, the Cherokee Constitution required approval of new tribal amendments by the Secretary of the Interior—the head of the same federal agency that attempted to wipe out the Cherokee Nation's government. The 2003 general election included a tribal constitutional referendum. Smith's administration presented Cherokee citizens with an opportunity to vote to approve a tribal amendment removing federal

---

5. Indeed, Jon Velie's pro bono civil rights career launched when the lawsuit he and is team filed on behalf of Seminole Freedmen in the U.S. courts was ruled in their favor. To Velie and other advocates, it was a win. But today, 13 years later, it is also perceived as a loss. "Does racism exist? Of course it does," Jon Velie said. "But this is legal racism." And to Velie, the implications of the ongoing Cherokee Nation litigation extend from Tahlequah to Wewoka and across Indian country.

13

approval of *future* amendments. To fellow Cherokee, it was an easy sell. If American Indian tribes are truly sovereign, what business is it of the U.S. government to approve their constitutional amendments?

But Smith still needed federal approval for such an amendment. That May, in addition to voting for Chief Smith, the majority of Cherokee citizens—excluding the Freedmen—had just voted in favor of the constitutional amendment. This was not enough to win over Department of Interior officials. Senior members within that federal agency realized the implications of approving such a measure—one that would forever forfeit their veto power over changes to the Cherokee tribal constitution. That same summer, the Department of Interior received alarming letters from Jon Velie; he warned of legal action should the Department of Interior fail to "honor its treaty obligations," and enforce the voting and citizenship rights of Cherokee Freedmen descendants.

The feds were now apprehensive. They worried that approving the amendment to remove oversight of future amendments would equip the Cherokee Nation—much like the Seminole Nation had a few years earlier—with the legal framework to turn around and remove their Freedmen by constitutional amendment.[6] Still, there were deeper tensions at play. After centuries of federal encroachment over tribal affairs, the Department of Interior labored to implement a policy that provided greater sovereign power to tribes, not less. The feds sought to strike a balance between providing more autonomy to Indian Nations and protecting the civil rights of Freedmen descendants. It was a tenuous balance at best.

In a letter to Chief Smith, Neal McCaleb, assistant secretary of the Department of Interior at the time, expressed the federal government's willingness to approve the amendment under the following conditions:

> All members of the Cherokee Nation, including the Freedman descendants who are otherwise qualified, must be provided an equal opportunity to vote in the election. Second, under current law, no amendment to the Nation's Constitution can eliminate the Freedmen from membership in the Nation absent Congressional authorization.

---

6. These sentiments emerged in the exchange of letters written by officials from the Department of Interior to Chief Smith and the Cherokee Nation.

FROM ONE FIRE

While serving as Cherokee Nation Principal Chief, and after he was defeated in 2011 by challenger, Bill John Baker, Chad Smith refused multiple requests to be interviewed for this story.[7] An examination of the letters he wrote over the last decade, court documents, and his speeches illustrate that Smith's stance toward Cherokee Freedmen descendants is unambiguous. In response to the Department of Interior's letter, Smith assured the federal government that citizenship rights would not be affected by the tribal constitutional amendment. Smith responded to Department of Interior:

> Nothing in the pending Constitutional Amendment will substantively alter in any manner whatsoever existing rules under the 1976 Constitution governing citizenship in the Cherokee Nation.

Smith was not being disingenuous, but he was not being forthcoming either. Though he did not say so at the time, Smith had always held the position that it was the original intention of 1976 Tribal Constitution—the most recently ratified Cherokee constitution at the time—to remove Freedmen citizenship. Smith, who was a trained lawyer and had recently spent a semester teaching Indian law at Dartmouth College, kept quiet on the issue. The Cherokee Nation's highest court would later disagree with Smith's interpretation.

In May 2003, the Cherokee Nation held its tribal elections. The tribal constitutional amendment to remove federal approval of future tribal amendments was placed on the ballot. The majority of the Cherokee Nation's citizens voted in favor of the amendment. Also, Chief Smith was elected to his second term in office. The Cherokee Freedmen, however, were not permitted to vote in this election.

That summer, the Department of Interior, Jon Velie, and Chief Smith exchanged a flurry of letters. To Smith, the controversy over the

---

7. When Smith was still chief he said through a spokesperson that he could not comment on the case because it was currently being litigated. I later approached him personally, he refused to answer my questions regarding the case. After he lost the tribal election, I called his private law office and left multiple messages with his secretary requesting an interview. He did not return my calls.

tribal citizenship rights for Freedmen descendants was an internal tribal issue. At stake was the Cherokee Nation's right to self-determination. When the Department of Interior officials directly questioned Smith's interpretation of the tribal constitution, and expressed reluctance to approve the tribal amendment removing its federal veto powers, Smith's tone grew more antagonistic. Smith wrote back to the Department of Interior:

> In the age of self-determination and self-governance, I am shocked to find the contents and tone of your letter to be both patronizing and very paternalistic. It appears that some officials in your department desire to return to the era of "bureaucratic imperialism."... It is a fact that the Cherokee people have decided their leadership and approved a constitutional amendment on May 24, 2003, by a democratic process in accordance with Cherokee Law.

Velie saw it differently.[8] However, the Department of Interior ultimately caved. Near summer's end in 2003, the Department of Interior formally recognized Smith as Chief of the Cherokee Nation for his second term—despite the Freedmen's exclusion at the polls. They did not, however, approve the tribal amendment removing federal approval of future tribal amendments. Nevertheless, on August 11, 2003, on behalf of Marilyn Vann, Kenneth Payton, Rodslen Brown-King, and other Freedmen descendants, Jon Velie filed a lawsuit in District Court against the Secretary of Interior, claiming that Smith was elected as chief without the Freedmen vote, in violation of the 1866 Treaty.

Cornsilk, paradoxically, was not pleased to learn about the lawsuit. Make no mistake, Cornsilk was vehemently opposed to the Cherokee Nation's exclusion of their Freedmen. But it is difficult to overstate just how deeply Cornsilk's Cherokee nationalistic sentiments run. Cornsilk was—and generally remains—against involving the federal government in tribal affairs. Velie's maneuvering, meanwhile, was strategic. Velie did

---

8. Velie felt that all elections that took place in 2003 were illegal because the Freedmen were not permitted to vote. Velie wanted the elections invalidated.

FROM ONE FIRE

not file suit directly against the Cherokee Nation. Such an approach, as the Nero case illustrated, risked early dismissal. Instead, Velie filed suit against the Department of Interior in an attempt to compel the federal agency to enforce treaty obligations over the Cherokee Nation. But to Cornsilk, the Cherokee Nation had been betrayed by federal government too many times to justify their present-day involvement.

When Cornsilk received the call and invitation from Vann to address the Freedmen descendants, he appeared after a day's work at Petsmart. The meeting took place at the Rudisill Regional Library, located in a predominately black neighborhood in north Tulsa, though within Cherokee Nation boundaries. "This woman stands up and talks about how she was mistreated by the Cherokee Nation," Cornsilk said. She said that Cherokee Nation officials had abused her because she appears black. The woman speaking was clad in formal dress and an old-fashioned hat. Her name is Lucy Allen. Cornsilk then stood up and addressed the room. He spoke of Roger Nero and Bernice Riggs. He also expressed his contempt for Chief Smith and his removal of the Freedmen. After the meeting, Lucy Allen pulled Cornsilk aside. Allen asked Cornsilk what could be done to combat Chief Smith.

"Let's sue," Cornsilk told Allen. Of course, he was talking about tribal court.

"I don't know what came over me. I was overcome with emotion, and concern for her, the Freedmen, and the future of my tribe," Cornsilk said.

It took nearly a year for his Petsmart colleagues to realize that Cornsilk was actively litigating on behalf of Lucy Allen and Cherokee Freedmen descendants outside of work hours.

"Whenever I had free time, I worked on the Freedmen case," Cornsilk said. At first, Cornsilk did not own a computer. He ended up purchasing one after securing a line of credit with Dell. He named his personal computer "Cherokee War Machine."

Early attempts by Cornsilk's opponents to dismiss the tribal case on various technicalities were unsuccessful. At least two out of the three tribal judges did not wish to see a tribal constitutional case dismissed on anything but the case's merits. "I would say that I didn't have a personal life," Cornsilk said. "My life was the case."

17

Cornsilk was a registered tribal lay advocate, working on behalf of Lucy Allen, so the majority of the court awarded Cornsilk a wide breadth of latitude—similar to one who represents oneself in court.

"I didn't try to twist anything or dazzle anyone with fancy words," Cornsilk said.

As Cornsilk pushed through early stages of the case, the Department of Interior took notice, as did the Justice Department. Cornsilk's tribal court case threatened Velie's ongoing litigation in the U.S. court system. The two cases more or less concerned the same issue. Through the lens of outsiders, Cornsilk's lawsuit supplied credence and legitimacy to Cherokee Nation tribal courts.[9]

Velie realized that Cornsilk's tribal suit supplied new ammunition for Smith's response to the feds. Smith had always argued that the Cherokee Nation had its own court system intact. In letters and briefs filed by the Cherokee Nation seeking early dismissal of Velie's suit, Smith often cited the older Nero case. Smith and his administration argued that the proper venue for the Freedmen grievances was indeed in tribal court. And no sooner did Cornsilk bring the Lucy Allen petition forward did Velie urge Cornsilk to drop the case. There was too much at stake. Also, as Cornsilk began litigating in tribal court, more obvious risks emerged. Cornsilk worked at Petsmart. What could he possibly know about tribal law? If Cornsilk lost—and most experts expected him to do so—it could thwart success of future litigation. What's more, Chief Smith had appointed the majority of tribal judges to the Cherokee Nation's highest court. Few expected Cornsilk to prevail.

And then there was the issue of Cornsilk's opponents. Cornsilk's preliminary research led him to believe that his best tactic was to file the Lucy Allen lawsuit against the Cherokee Nation Tribal Council, which functions as the tribe's legislative body. Cornsilk argued that the

---

9. Like the federal government and states, federally recognized tribes normally enjoy general immunity from lawsuits. For petitioners like the Freedmen, this often leaves no other option but to sue in tribal courts. In Roger Nero's case, which was in essence, a civil rights case, Nero attempted to sue in US Courts over his right to vote in a tribal election. But his petition was too narrow and focused on the particulars of tribal registration policy. As a consequence, a judge held that permitting the case to be decided in US Courts would curb the tribe's capacity to "maintain itself as a culturally and politically distinct entity." It ruled that the proper jurisdiction for Nero's suit was in tribal court.

new Cherokee Nation requirement that determined tribal citizenship link to the "by blood" subsection of the Dawes Rolls was extra-constitutional, and therefore unconstitutional. At the time, one of the tribal council's longtime members—with greater political ambitions—was Bill John Baker. The tribal council selected their attorney to defend Cornsilk's petition: a young rising Cherokee Nation tribal lawyer, Todd Hembree.

Velie was correct to worry about Cornsilk's tribal court filing. It would emerge later in a congressional investigation that the feds perceived the Cherokee Freedmen differently than the Seminole Freedmen case. In the Seminole case, Jon Velie's legal team had already convinced the federal government to force the Seminole Nation to reinstate citizenship rights to its Freedmen descendants, or forfeit federal funding, and with it, a license to operate lucrative casinos. The Department of Interior later told members of Congress that they involved themselves in the Seminole Freedmen case because, unlike the Cherokee Nation, the Seminole Nation did not have an adequate tribal court system in place. The Cherokee Nation did, and as the tribal case dragged on, Cornsilk helped prove it.

As Cornsilk's case reached its final stages, Hembree and Cornsilk filed motions almost daily.

"I threw everything in except the kitchen sink," Cornsilk said.

On March 7, 2006, nine months after Cornsilk's closing arguments, a tribal court clerk placed a call to Petsmart. One of Cornsilk's colleagues paged him over the loudspeaker. Cornsilk was unloading dog food from a truck bed out back and missed the page. The colleague tracked down Cornsilk and informed him that he had a call. When Cornsilk lifted the phone, Lisa Fields, the court clerk asked Cornsilk if he was sitting down.

"No," Cornsilk replied. "Should I be?"'

"You won," she told him. "You won the Freedmen lawsuit."

"My knees got weak and I felt myself get faint," he recalled.

Cornsilk asked Fields to fax over the decision. Petsmart staff packed around the office watching the fax machine spit out pages.

"They were like, 'There's another one,' " he said. "Everything I had done: writing the letter to Wilma Mankiller, standing there with Nero, everything flashed before my eyes."

Petsmart later promoted Cornsilk to assistant manager.

Marcos Barbery

BENDING THE WILL OF A PEOPLE

The day after David Cornsilk defeated Hembree in tribal court, he received a congratulatory call from an official at the U.S. Justice Department. Two weeks later, Chief Smith issued a memorandum to the Cherokee Nation registrar:

"With no requirement for proof of Cherokee blood, certain Registration procedures must necessarily be adjusted accordingly," Smith wrote. "Applications from prospective citizens without Cherokee blood are to be processed on the same basis as all other applications for citizenship."

In light of the Lucy Allen decision, Smith instructed senior tribal leaders to revise forms, brochures, and to inform other staff of the implications of the tribal court's decision. "I thought it was over," Cornsilk said, "but I underestimated the racism of Chad Smith." In a letter Smith would later write to members of Congress, he denied that the following events were motivated by racial prejudice.

Cornsilk's victory, however, was accompanied by a curious opinion. Stacy Leeds, then a Cherokee tribal court justice, wrote the majority decision, the precise wording of which armed Smith's administration and their supporters with new leverage. Leeds narrowly wrote that there is no "clear language in the 1976 Cherokee Constitution to exclude the Freedman from citizenship." However, Leeds also noted that the Cherokee citizenry has the ultimate authority to define tribal citizenship, but they "must do so expressly:"

> If the Cherokee people wish to limit tribal citizenship, and such limitation would terminate the pre-existing citizenship of even one Cherokee citizen, then it must be done in the open. It cannot be accomplished through silence.

It was around these few sentences that Smith and his supporters would stage a new strategy. Smith proposed passing a tribal constitutional amendment on Freedmen citizenship through public referendum. This presented a chance, Smith claimed, for Cherokee citizens to vote—in the open—to overturn the result of the tribal court's decision.

FROM ONE FIRE

"The issue at hand is what classes[10] of people should be citizens of the Cherokee Nation, and who should make that decision, the courts or the Cherokee people themselves," Smith said during his 2006 State of the Nation address, after the Allen decision. "The process to decide the issue of Freedmen citizenship is a constitutional amendment at the polls."

With another election for Principal Chief looming, Smith faced an important year. Smith's third-term as Principal Chief was at stake, and he and his supporters acted swiftly. Almost immediately after the tribal court decision, Smiths' supporters and anti-Freedmen advocates advanced a tribal petition. Their goal was to garner enough signatures to bring forth a referendum at the polls. Cornsilk countered by launching an aggressive campaign to register new Freedmen. As a result of Cornsilk's tribal court win, Cherokee citizenship rights had been restored to Freedmen descendants. Cornsilk and Vann's efforts helped secure Cherokee citizenship to about 2,800 Freedmen descendants. Though they didn't know it at the time, the window for Freedmen descendants to apply for tribal citizenship was closing.

Velie contends that after the Allen decision, Smith and his administration set out to increase the size of the Cherokee Nation's then-highest court. The Allen case had been decided by three judges in a 2-to-1 decision, with Stacy Leeds writing for the majority. After the Allen decision, Smith appointed two new members to the court and renamed it: The Cherokee Supreme Court. During a rare public debate, Velie said that Smith intentionally "dismantled the court" to exert tighter control over its decisions. Smith interrupted Velie's allotted time to say, "That's not true." Stacy Leeds contends that court expansion plans were set in motion before Smith became chief. Leeds said that the court's expansion had no correlation to the Freedmen issue. Nevertheless, the court's expansion would play a critical role in a lawsuit Cornsilk would file next.

In late 2006, David Cornsilk, Marilyn Vann, and other volunteers began inspecting various signatures gathered by petition leaders. Cornsilk and Vann discovered inconsistencies, and what they believed were

---

10. Here, Chief Smith's choice of word ("classes") is laced in racial undertones. It is precisely this kind of tone and choice of wording that caused many Freedmen to feel offended by Chief Smith's political rhetoric.

fraudulent signatories. Cornsilk once more filed suit in tribal court challenging the authenticity of the various petitions. The recently expanded tribal court invalidated some signatures, but overall ruled against Cornsilk. Stacy Leeds, in this case, wrote a lone dissenting opinion calling the petition glaringly fraudulent.

That December, Stacy Leeds's term as tribal justice expired. Chief Smith did not appoint her to an additional term. In January 2007, Leeds launched a campaign to run for chief of the Cherokee Nation against Chad Smith in the forthcoming general election. Leeds, who had supported Smith in a prior campaign, said that Smith lost all objectivity and was not listening to or considering different perspectives. "There were subtle abuses of power occurring at many levels in the government," Leeds wrote in an email. "But the idea that a sitting Principal Chief would orchestrate a popular vote to overturn a ruling of the Nation's highest court and thereby strip a group of Cherokee citizens of their legal rights is a good example of why new leadership was necessary."

With the petition's 2,100 signatures now authenticated by the Cherokee Nation's highest court and the tribal council, the date for the special constitutional amendment was set for March 3, 2007—just several months before an already scheduled general election. On this day, out of the 8,000 Cherokee citizens who cast votes, over three-quarters voted in favor of permanently excluding Cherokee Freedman descendants from tribal citizenship.[11] The nearly 2,800 Freedmen who were permitted to vote during the special election fell short of a victory. Nearly one year later to the day, Cornsilk's victory was overturned.

Three weeks later, the Cherokee Nation tribal registrar issued letters to Freedmen descendants: "We regret to inform you that you are not

---

11. During an interview with Todd Hembree, I asked if the 2007 Cherokee constitutional amendment that overturned Cornsilk's landmark tribal ruling and removed the Cherokee Freedmen was political. Hembree said that he is a realist. "It wasn't a mere coincidence that we had a special election in March of 2007 when there was a general election a few months later." But then he revealed that after years fighting against Cornsilk in tribal court and losing, during the 2007 special election he personally voted against the constitutional amendment that removed the Freedmen. "I did not vote for that petition, but that is my right as an individual," Hembree said. "Now, when the Cherokee people speak in overwhelming percentages, that's who I represent."

eligible for citizenship in the Cherokee Nation." Six days later, another letter was issued to each enrolled Cherokee Freedmen descendant. "This letter is to inform you that because of the Constitutional Amendment, you are no longer eligible to receive health services through Cherokee Nation," the Cherokee Nation's clinic administrator wrote. Two months later, Stacy Leeds lost in the general election to incumbent Chief Smith. She is now dean of the law school at the University of Arkansas.

"With only four months to put a campaign together with zero dollars in an initial campaign fund, we came very close to unseating a two-term incumbent," Leeds said. Nearly twice as many Cherokee voted in the general election compared to the special election.

RACE AND POLITICS

Later that summer, in Washington, D.C., Representative Diane Watson, D-Los Angeles, caught wind of the Cherokee Freedmen's disenrollment. At the time, Representative Watson served on the Congressional Black Caucus. After studying the case, meeting with Freedmen and their advocates, and checking the veracity of their statements with officials at Bureau of Indian Affairs, Watson drafted legislation.

From the moment Watson began seeking co-sponsors to the bill, the Cherokee Nation unleashed a comprehensive response. The bill's scope and substance was sweeping and unequivocal. Its purpose was to "sever the United States relations with the Cherokee Nation of Oklahoma until the Cherokee Nation restored the rights of the Freedman." Congressman Mel Watt, D-North Carolina, who like Watson is black, co-sponsored the bill. "Once I reviewed the facts and the background information and history," Congressman Watt said, "You don't turn and look the other way."

With hundreds of millions of federal dollars on the line, and millions more at stake related to its gaming license,[12] the Cherokee Nation applied extensive resources to its defense. Jack Abramoff, the Cherokee Nation's former lobbyist—who was hired by Chief Smith to lobby on behalf of "sovereignty issues," and who personally contributed to Smith's campaign for Cherokee Principal Chief—was serving time in federal prison on unrelated convictions. The Cherokee Nation's hired external lobbyists, Tony Podesta of the Podesta Group and brother of John Podesta, who was White House Chief of Staff in the Clinton Administration, and Lanny Davis, special counsel to President Clinton during his impeachment proceedings and now a D.C.-based lobbyist. The Cherokee Nation's D.C. team applied primary pressure against Congress.

Officially, Podesta concentrated on battling against the proposed bill while Davis focused most of his energy on the ongoing Vann case. In practice, Davis also helped the Cherokee Nation lobby Congress to kill Watson's proposed bill. As a former attorney to President Clinton, Davis is well connected in Washington—connected to a degree his fees reflect. "The Cherokee Nation put on a full court press," explained Bert Hammond, principal advisor to Representative Watson. "I'm sure that their law firm got paid millions and millions of dollars to lobby on their behalf."[13] As part of its policy, the Podesta Group does not discuss its relationships with current or former clients, and Lanny Davis did not respond to interview requests.

---

12. Cherokee Nation's chief concern, according to interviews, was that the bill threatened the tribe's license to operate casinos. At the time, gaming made up the majority of the tribe's business arm's $520 million in annual revenue. Curiously, members of Congress who ultimately co-supported the bill were unaware that the Cherokee Nation's business arm, then known as Cherokee Industries, was engaged in manufacturing contracts with the Department of Defense. Also, according to a senior official within the Cherokee's business arm, had the Watson bill become law, the tribe's defense contracts would have remained intact, though this seems unlikely.
13. According to public filings, the Podesta Group, a registered lobbying group, earned $60,000 per year for their directly lobbying efforts and certainly much more for "counsel" and "advice". However, because Lanny Davis was hired as an attorney, as opposed to a lobbyist, his fee remains unknown. He has been rumored to charge $600 per hour.

Watson, and other members of the Black Caucus introduced the bill, which was submitted in 2008 to the House Natural Resources and House Judiciary committees. The National NAACP supported the bill, framing the Cherokee Nation's 2007 constitutional amendment as racist. Smith rejected the "inflammatory misrepresentations" against the tribe. "The 2007 vote to amend its constitution was a crucial vote for the future of the Cherokee Nation and its own sense of identity," Smith wrote to members of Congress. "This vote has been falsely characterized as racist, while, in fact, the vote was for an explicit clarification of who is a documented Indian in regards to citizenship in the Cherokee Nation."

Podesta and Davis, along with Paula Ragsdale,[14] the Cherokee Nation's in-house D.C.-based lobbyist at the time, argued that the bill's central issue was currently under judicial review by U.S. Appeals Court and District Court of Washington, D.C. Cherokee lobbyists now felt that U.S. courts were best positioned to rule on the issue. Nearly five years after filing, the Vann case had not yet reached the merits stage.

Watson eventually changed the bill's language so that it would be referred to the judiciary committee. The change was strategic because John Conyers, another member of the Black Caucus, chaired the committee at the time. It was expected that as a representative known for his leadership on civil rights issues, Conyers would lend his support to the Freedmen. But the bill failed to gather steam. Asked why the bill was eventually killed, Hammond replied, "my clinical reaction is that the Cherokee chief had been around here spreading money around," he said. "And they have money to spread around."[15]

---

14. Findings also suggest that relationships—which in this case extended even beyond the incestuous nature known for fueling D.C. politics—played a significant role in killing the proposed legislation. Pat Ragsdale, the then number three at the Bureau of Indian Affairs within the Department of Interior, is married to Paula Ragsdale, the Cherokee Nation's internal D.C. lobbyist.

15. During a 2011 public event in Tulsa marking the commemoration of the Tulsa Race Riots, then-Chief Smith responded to accusations of tribal racism targeting blacks by showing the audience a video recording of a speech John Conyers delivered at the tribe's headquarters in 2009. The substance of Conyers' speech focused on the Trail of Tears; he did not mention the Freedmen. It is presumed that Smith hoped Conyers' presence at the Cherokee Nation alone was vindication.

Members of Congress, including Barney Frank, a Massachusetts representative at the time known for backing civil rights issues, lobbied the U.S. Justice Department to take action against the Cherokee Nation. The Podesta Group made similar appeals, this time before the Obama administration. On April 30, 2009, Representative Watson submitted a letter to U.S. Attorney General Eric Holder requesting that the Justice Department's Civil Rights Division open an investigation into the "plight of the Freedman" and Smith's "illegal elections." Holder did not respond until nearly four months later—that is, after President Obama appointed Kimberly Teehee, a Cherokee, as his Senior Policy Advisor for Native American Affairs. On August 12, 2009, Holder notified members of Congress of his unwillingness to open a civil rights investigation on Smith. Holder cited the pending Vann case in U.S. courts.

THE JURY WITHIN

To ascend to the main floor of the National Lincoln Memorial in Washington, D.C., Marilyn Vann, who suffers from health problems, required the assistance of an elevator. To reach it on a cool night this past October, Vann shuffled uneasily through a corridor beneath the memorial. The corridor doubles as a museum illustrating critical events that shaped the Civil Rights Movement. Walls are etched in black and white portraits of Dr. Martin Luther King, Jr., whose "I Have a Dream" speech crackled over loud speakers. Vann's attorney, Jon Velie, joined her. The next morning, nearly a decade after they first filed their lawsuit, the two were once again due in federal court. But tonight, Vann wished to set her eyes on the memorial depicting the former president. Once at the top, the elevator's doors drew open like stage curtains. When Lincoln's statue revealed itself drenched in light, Vann, who had been chatting with Velie, fell silent.

From the outside, it is difficult to understand why the Vann case has yet to be argued on its merits. It is helpful to think about the case not as two parties on the same playing field seeking to right a wrong, but rather one party demanding that one country apply its laws or treaties over another. The case continues to unravel at a glacial pace because to the Cherokee Nation, its supreme authority to self-determination is at stake. Perhaps nobody understands this better than David

FROM ONE FIRE

Cornsilk. In spite of his staunch role advocating on behalf of the Freedmen, Cornsilk believes that each time the Cherokee Nation is dragged into a U.S. court, the tribe's sovereignty is diminished.[16] Cornsilk blames the Cherokee Nation for exposing the tribe—and potentially establishing a dangerous precedent for all American Indian nations—over what he calls an unequivocal repression of the Cherokee Freedmen descendants' tribal rights. Cornsilk says that there is simply no other option than to pursue justice in U.S. courts. To Cornsilk, the only hope for the Freedmen's chance of regaining their tribal citizenship hinges on the work of Vann and Velie.

At the U.S. Federal Court of Appeals hearing the morning after Vann and Velie visited the Lincoln Memorial, those anticipating a resolution were sorely disappointed. As Jon Velie's and Todd Hembree's legal teams argued before three white federal appellate judges, there was a sense that something historical was unfolding. But nobody—not even the local law students who crowded near the front of the courtroom—seemed to have a firm grasp of what was occurring. "To me, that was all legal mumbo jumbo," a Freedmen descendant who lives in Washington, D.C., told me after the hearing. The lawyers argued over whether the chief of the Cherokee Nation could be named as a defendant—or in legal jargon, if *Ex parte Young* applies to the Cherokee Nation. Two months later, in December, the court ruled in favor of the Freedmen, delivering a blow to the Cherokee Nation and a victorious jolt to Vann, Velie, and Freedmen advocates.

The Vann case may now proceed, but in spite of the latest Freedmen victory, the case could drag on for years to come. In one instance, the Cherokee Nation could appeal this latest decision—a legal procedural decision—to the U.S. Supreme Court. It's an attractive option. So far, the Cherokee Nation's legal maneuvering has succeeded in stalling the Vann case. "The Cherokee Nation says that it wants this case to be settled, but what they're really doing is delaying," Velie said, "while over 90 percent of the Freedmen are denied citizenship." And at least in one glaringly

---

16. Though they share similarities, Native American tribes are not states. They are semi-autonomous nations with inherent sovereign rights. "Without sovereignty, we're nothing more than a Kiwanis club or a Rotary club," Todd Hembree said.

obvious way, even if Velie's team were to ultimately win the case, they have already lost. The Cherokee Freedmen descendants remain disenfranchised. It is no surprise then that nearly two years into his tenure, Freedmen descendants have grown increasingly disillusioned by Smith's successor: Principal Chief Bill John Baker.

While Baker was still running for Chief of the Cherokee Nation and serving as a member of the Cherokee Nation Tribal Council, he agreed to sit down with me at his campaign headquarters. Baker's campaign occupied a front office within Baker Furniture—a sprawling warehouse store he owns along Tahlequah's main drag. Outside, a red, white, and blue two-story banner depicting Baker's image fluttered against a breeze. I said to Baker that the majority of Cherokee Nation leadership positions appear to be filled by white-appearing Cherokee citizens. "Well, we've never been a tribe of full-bloods," Baker said. When I mentioned that historians suggest that Freedmen descendants may have more Cherokee blood running through them than white-appearing "by-blood" Cherokee, Baker conceded that it wasn't fair.

"Why don't you and the tribal council change policy?" I asked.

"It is not fair," Baker said. "But it is our way."[17]

Advocates say, however, that during his campaign, Baker positioned himself politically as an ally to the Freedmen cause only to later betray them after he won. Indeed, his rise to the tribe's highest office was a consequence of the Freedmen vote, they say. Today, under federal agreement, only a small fraction of potential Cherokee Freedmen are permitted to vote in tribal elections. These are the 2,800 Freedmen descendants who successfully registered during the year-long window following Cornsilk's tribal court victory and the tribal constitutional referendum that stripped it away. This highly limited number of Freedmen descendants are permitted to vote in tribal elections under an agreement between U.S. Congress, the Department of Interior, and the Cherokee Nation—while the Vann case plays out in U.S. courts.

In the June 2011 general tribal election, in which incumbent Chief Smith campaigned for his fourth term, it was first reported that Baker beat Smith by a handful of votes. Given Smith's 12-year posture toward

---

17. Since last year's election, Chief Baker has turned down requests to be interviewed.

FROM ONE FIRE

Freedmen descendants, advocates say that the fraction of potential Freedmen descendants who were permitted to vote supported Baker as a block—handing Baker an edge. The Cherokee Nation's highest court later ruled that the June 2011 tribal election results were too close to call. Another general election was scheduled for that September. Then, in August, just three weeks before the newly scheduled special election, the same tribal court ruled to strip the voting rights of the marginal 2,800 Cherokee Freedmen descendants—in apparent violation of the federal agreement. Baker, joining the side of Freedmen advocates, was outraged. After all, without the fractional Freedmen vote, the election would have no doubt once again swung in Smith's favor.

After Representative Frank and his colleagues protested, the federal government froze tens of millions of dollars in U.S. taxpayer funds scheduled for distribution to the Cherokee Nation that fall. An emergency U.S. court hearing took place in Washington, D.C., days before the September election. The ruling—another Velie victory—led to the reinstatement of voting rights to the limited 2,800 Freedmen. The public relations damage to Smith and his administration surged. Smith never recovered. Baker ended up winning the special general election by an even wider margin.[18] Now, thrust into his second year as chief, as the Vann case drags on,[19] the hopes held among Freedmen descendants that Baker would drop the U.S. court case and support their cause have all but evaporated.

Many of those sentiments have served to only strengthen the case against the Cherokee Nation within the court of public opinion. It is here that the Cherokee Nation may be fighting a losing battle. Each time the Vann case twists and turns, the tribe is forced into the public relations

---

18. "Let's hope that the new chief has a better attitude," Congressman Watt said. "And if he doesn't, we'll fight the new chief just like we did Chief Smith." Freedmen advocates, particularly David Cornsilk, have been disappointed in the apparent reluctance of members of Congress to take action to support the Freedmen cause.

19. Today, the Cherokee Nation argues that the 1866 Treaty guaranteed membership rights to Freedmen and their descendants. In 1867, the Cherokee Nation amended their tribal constitution to include the word "citizenship" rights to their Freedmen. Now, the tribe says that it had a sovereign right to do so, just as it had an equal right to amend their constitution nearly 150 years later to remove their Freedmen descendants by tribal constitutional amendment. The tribe supports the 1866 Treaty, but believes there is a distinction between membership rights and citizenship rights.

MARCOS BARBERY

quagmire that comes with defending against a decade-long lawsuit in which race—at least appears—to play a critical role. For years, Freedmen advocacy journalists and bloggers have vilified the tribe and its leaders with little balance, framing the Cherokee leaders and citizens as racists. In cases where race is the central question of law, this court tends to favor the plaintiffs.[20]

On the ground in Tahlequah, there are signs emerging that the entrenched division surrounding the Freedmen controversy that once so heavily blanketed the Cherokee Nation is slowly receding. Cherokee citizens have grown undoubtedly more docile, and in many cases, supportive of the Freedmen. "I think they have a right to claim citizenship," a teenage full-blood Cherokee told me after a powwow. Perhaps unfairly, fear of appearing racist—even if race is not, in fact, a factor—has taken a stronger hold. This may help explain why Corey Still, the University of Oklahoma full-blood Cherokee, had a change of heart. After the public debate in Norman, when the floor opened for questions, Still aggressively cross-examined Jon Velie from the audience. When I approached Still afterwards and introduced myself as a journalist and filmmaker, he agreed to share his personal feelings about the Freedmen during a formal interview. Months later, Still changed his mind.

Cornsilk attributes any changing tide, however slight, not to the tribe's public relations woes or new strategy, but to education. He says that the case has helped reveal the truth about the Cherokee Freedmen to the rest of the tribe. Many Cherokee who did vote against the Freedmen in 2007 are regretful of doing so now, he said. "Overcoming racism

---

20. Where Baker has largely fallen silent on the Freedmen controversy since taking office, Todd Hembree has spoken openly about the case. In doing so, Hembree is leading the official shift in tone toward the Cherokee Freedmen—from the top down. It is an important front in the tribe's new public relations strategy. Gone is the combative tone toward Cherokee Freedmen that helped define the Smith administration. Hembree has helped replace it with a sense of transparency and civility, while still doggedly litigating against Velie and the Freedmen's claims. The night before the Cherokee Nation Tribal parade—as Rodslen Brown-King and her family wheeled the Freedmen float into place for the next morning's festivities—Hembree dined with the owners of one of Tahlequah's finer dining establishments. Comfortable in a dark suit, seemingly earnest, and at ease rubbing shoulders with Tahlequah's elite, it's hard not to see Hembree for his own political ambitions. He looks like a lot like a chief waiting in the wings.

FROM ONE FIRE

is a long process," Cornsilk said. He believes that if another constitutional referendum took place today, while close, the Freedmen would be welcomed back into the tribe. What Cornsilk and Velie have achieved through their legal advocacy—from within and outside the tribe respectively—is given voice to Freedmen descendants like Lucy Allen and Marilyn Vann. And if part of their goal is to force more Cherokee to confront their own stained history with slavery, and move closer toward tribal reconciliation, then no matter the outcome of the Vann case, they are winning.

Velie is less optimistic, not about the potential of the Cherokee people to support the Freedmen, but of their tribal political leaders to abstain from leveraging race for political gains. Velie says that, at present, the vast majority of the Cherokee Freedmen still cannot vote or run for tribal office. He is charging on. If Velie is ultimately successful in the U.S. courts, one person now poised to help process Freedmen descendants—like Kenneth Payton[21] and Rodslen Brown-King and their children—as newly minted Cherokee citizens is none other than David Cornsilk. This January, Chief Bill John Baker hired David Cornsilk to return to work within the Cherokee Nation Registration Office. There was one condition. Cornsilk would have to cease from publicly criticizing the tribe's position toward its Freedmen descendants. When the job was first offered, Cornsilk was still living in his car. Regardless, Cornsilk refused to sign the gag order. In need of a talented genealogist—or perhaps in the execution of the long-tested political strategy of keeping

---

21. On an overcast afternoon last spring at Kenneth Payton's home in Broken Arrow, he flipped through a series of family photographs. "To be included and to feel included would change the whole dynamic," he said. As Payton's sons horsed around upstairs, I asked Payton if his children understood their heritage. "The younger ones, if somebody came up to them they would say, 'Yeah, I'm Indian," he said. On the surface, Payton appears black, and Hembree white, but draw in closer and gradations emerge. For all of their divisiveness, Freedmen and Cherokee officials share one common purpose: closing the gap between how they perceive themselves from the within, and how they are perceived from the outside.

MARCOS BARBERY

friends close, enemies closer—the Cherokee Nation hired Cornsilk anyway. Cornsilk has since moved into a new apartment.

YOUNGWOLFE ACCUSED

An Atticus Finch story set in Tulsa County

BY *Hunter Howe Cates*

PHYLLIS JEAN WARREN WAS MISSING FOR THREE WEEKS when she was found strangled in a brush pile 300 yards from her home. Wrenched around her swollen neck was her blue plastic belt and stuffed in her pocket were her own blood-stained panties. It was April 2, 1953. She was 11. It was a short hunt before the police found their man in Warren's neighbor, a 21-year-old Cherokee Indian named Buster Young-wolfe. Childlike himself despite being a husband and father, Buster was always friendly with his gleeful neighbor, no doubt suspecting he was the object of her adolescent affections. Already on probation for a botched burglary committed in his teens, he'd twice lied about his alibi for March 12, the night Phyllis disappeared. First he told the police he was at the movies. Then he admitted he was out drinking.

After five days and nights in a Tulsa County jailhouse, Youngwolfe broke. Re-enacting the crime, he confessed to taking Phyllis out to a field, crushing her jaw, then raping her. When she threatened to tell his wife, he covered her mouth until she stopped moving. Not sure if she was dead, he unfastened her belt and strangled what life she had left. He then dug a hole with his bare hands and buried her body in the brush.

Her daddy did always warn her to stay away from that Indian man.

The police made an announcement and all that remained was the formality of a trial. A penniless roofer, Buster was assigned public defender named Elliott "Bill" Howe, only 33 and barely out of law school. Making $250 for 50 cases a month, he did this job part time without an office or secretary. But not much was needed for a case this cut and dried.

Attorney and client met the day Buster confessed. The case wasn't even discussed, as the two men shared a cigarette and not much else. But the next morning Buster called his lawyer and said it was urgent. Not sure what to expect, Bill arrived as soon as he could.

"You had something to tell me?" Bill asked.

"Yeah," Buster whispered, sticking his head through the bars. "I didn't do it."

But Buster had already confessed, which his lawyer pointed out.

"Sure I confessed," Buster said. "They worked on me for five days. I only had two meals. I only slept four hours." Besides, he was an ex-convict. Who'd believe him? The police told him the best he could hope for was a life sentence. Otherwise, he'd die in the chair.

Skeptical, Bill called in a reporter friend and the two grilled Buster for three hours. The more they talked, the more Bill found himself believing in Youngwolfe's story.

"If you're lying now," Bill warned, "you will get the chair."

Buster's eyes widened. "I *didn't* do it."

Bill believed him. Most of Tulsa County didn't—or couldn't. But Bill did. By defending Buster, he would be risking his reputation, something he valued as much as anything in the world. But Bill was convinced he had an innocent man.

The murder of Phyllis Warren and trial of Buster Youngwolfe was a huge story in its day, receiving national coverage ranging from *Inside Detective* to *Redbook* and *Newsweek*. Unfortunately, that is now about the only place you will find it—dusty, old magazines. And with each passing year, those who remember it are lost to time. I am lucky. I know this story because Bill Howe was my grandfather.

To know why my grandfather fought for this young man, you have to know the journey that brought him there. Four years old when his white father died, eight when his Creek mother followed, Bill was sent off to Chilocco Indian School on the Kansas border. The only reason he went was because his well-bred Virginia relatives would take him—with

YOUNGWOLFE ACCUSED

his blond hair and blue eyes—but not his brown-skinned, raven-haired little brother.

My grandfather wouldn't have it. Despite his quarter-Creek blood, he found himself the only fair-skinned kid in the school. According to him, he got his nose bloodied three times the first day. The combined weight of poverty, bullying, and loneliness made him bitter and rebellious. His headmaster told him, "Howe, you'll be in the penitentiary before you're 21."

He may have been right. My grandfather could've become a Buster Youngwolfe. Ironically, it was this frigid comment that inspired him to prove the headmaster wrong. He set himself straight and became a lawyer, one in whose hands Buster had now placed his life.

Bill recognized in Buster the natural reticence he'd seen growing up around American Indians. His life at Chilocco, and among his own flesh and blood, taught him that even the most jovial among them could close off around those outside their group. Buster was no different, which made defending him difficult. The police were convinced he was hiding something.

Bill had no proof that Buster was innocent, except his word. That, and a gut feeling.

If Buster was convicted in the court of public opinion, Bill now hung next to him. Gossipmongers said he was just juicing up publicity, all the while defending a monster who had murdered a child. But my grandfather couldn't worry about that. There was too much work to do.

Truth was, Buster *had* lied about his alibi. He didn't go to the movies on March 12, but had spent the day scouring bars with his father and brother to celebrate his 21st birthday. Because drinking would've violated his probation, he lied to keep himself out of jail for two years.

Even after learning these facts, the sheriff never bothered to check the bars. Bill did, and found several waitresses who remembered seeing Buster. Buster's father also remembered a traffic ticket they received that night, proving they were out driving as they claimed.

Bill also examined the crime scene, where Buster confessed to digging Warren's grave with his bare hands. Even for a healthy young man like Buster, that would've been nearly impossible, as tightly packed as the dirt was. Finally, Bill visited Warren and Buster's neighborhood, though to call it such is a stretch. A morbid collection of two-room tar paper shacks, this slum was home to at least six sex offenders. None were ever questioned.

My grandfather kept the facts close to his chest, even as public opinion grew vicious. By now strangers and friends alike would walk on the other side of the street simply to avoid him.

To ensure there were no doubts about Buster's innocence, my grandfather petitioned for a lie detector test. At that time, the test could only be admitted as evidence if both sides agreed to it. County Prosecutor Robert L. Wheeler went along with Bill's "crazy idea."

The region's best administer of lie detector tests was Kansas City Police Captain Phil Hoyt, who, it was said, had never been proved wrong in 6,052 tests. Buster, joined by the county attorney, a handful of deputies, and Bill, was driven 243 miles for the test. It was agreed the results would not be revealed until Hoyt took the stand as the last witness of the trial.

My grandfather was confident in Buster's innocence and in the case he'd prepared. But the enormity of his responsibility was taking its toll. "I had convinced [Buster's] family I would get him free," he told *Redbook*. "They were sleeping nights. I wasn't."

His fears were unfounded. The county's case against Youngwolfe unraveled from the start. Waitresses testified to Buster's whereabouts on the night of March 12. Neighbors reported seeing him drunk when friends brought him home. On the stand, the sheriff admitted to pressuring him during his five-day incarceration. A local reporter even testified that Buster had confessed to him his innocence—a bombshell that never made it to print.

The trial was going in my grandfather's favor. But then in an instant, everything fell apart. Bill had placed great weight on the traffic fine as evidence that Buster and his family were out driving on March 12. However, the county attorney produced the document, showing it was dated March 13—the *day after* Phyllis disappeared. The one recorded piece of evidence supporting Buster's alibi crumbled.

The county's victory was short-lived. As the record book made its way through the jury, one juror pointed out that the dates had been changed. It *had* read "March 12", but had obviously been rewritten to "March 13." Buster's alibi stood.

Finally, Hoyt took the stand. He detailed his methods just shy of an hour, as silence and stifling heat swept the congested courtroom. Then he delivered his final statement. When he said he did not kill Phyllis Warren, Hoyt testified, "Buster Youngwolfe has been telling the truth."

———————————

The county attorney threw in the towel, telling the jury, "I cannot conscientiously ask you to convict this defendant."

"We knew you had it all the time!" friends told Bill, pretending they were on his side from the beginning. Politicians emerged, discussing this young defense attorney's prospects. Bill would have none of it.

"I'm no hero, and don't you forget it," he told *Redbook*. "I had an innocent man, and that's the most any attorney can ask."

This story was a natural sell for the national media—a heinous crime, a wrongfully accused man, a crusading attorney, all set in the wildcatting, cowboys-and-Indians landscape of Tulsa. Pulpy true detective magazines, which covered the story before the trial, treated it as a noir-ish tale of sordid crime, depicting with a flourish Youngwolfe as a cold-blooded savage. *Newsweek*, which ran the story after the trial, used the exotic title "Lie-Detector Indian," as if my grandfather possessed supernatural powers: half witch doctor, half defense attorney.

———————————

Justice is allegedly blind, but the court of public opinion follows no rules, now or in 1953. And, when the case involves a former felon and a murdered girl, the truth can be buried deeper than Phyllis Jean Warren ever could be.

My grandfather knew better. While, like any man, Bill Howe had his flaws, his trademark characteristic was an almost stubborn fairness. Certainly he understood how much he was risking in taking Youngwolfe's case. Even so, I suspect it simply never occurred to him not to. He had an innocent man to defend and didn't give a damn about the consequences, personal or professional. That sounds just like him.

Youngwolfe's fate is unknown to me, and tragically Phyllis Jean Warren's killer was never found. As for my grandfather, he never pursued politics, nor was there another Buster Youngwolfe in his career. What followed for him were two of the things he wanted most—a respected practice and a devoted family, like the one he lost as a boy. It was the latter that was by his side the day he died on January 21, 2007.

I don't know why my grandfather trusted Youngwolfe, a man most of the city had condemned before even the trial. Maybe he saw in him what he easily could have become himself: a life left behind simply because no one believed in him. Buster Youngwolfe deserved justice. He deserved a defense. In my grandfather, he found it.

WATTS AND CLARY

How an unlikely friendship developed between a black civil rights activist and a former Imperial Wizard of the White Knights of the KKK

By *Steve Gerkin*

Dressed only in his boxers, Wade Watts, a black civil rights activist reclined on the sofa. He read the morning paper while bacon, eggs, and pork sausage sizzled in the kitchen. The cook leaned into the living room doorway.

"Do you think your friend Martin Luther King, who dreamt that one day blacks and whites could come together, ever imagined it might include us?"

Johnny Lee Clary, former Imperial Wizard of the White Knights of the Ku Klux Klan, returned to the stove.

From the other room, Watts, an evangelist and longtime leader of the NAACP, shouted his answer.

"No," he said, "I don't believe the dream would have gone that far. But don't burn this couch after I leave, honky!"

A few years earlier, that may have been a possibility. While Johnny Lee was the Grand Dragon of the Oklahoma Klan, the Klan set fire to Watts' church, nearly burning it to the ground.

As the Grand Dragon of Oklahoma, Clary launched an all-out campaign of retribution against the disciple of love, the Reverend Watts. During a late-1970s radio debate in Oklahoma City, Watts tormented

Clary, citing scripture and sprinkling his rebuttals with "Jesus loves you." Embarrassed Klan protégées listened to the destruction of Johnny Lee.

Wade Watts was born in the hills of Kiamichi, southeast Oklahoma, in 1919. Indoctrinated into the teachings of the Baptist church at a young age, he committed his life to Christian ideals. At 17, Watts joined the NAACP. The organization elected him the state president in 1968, a position he held for 16 years. His respect within the civil rights community escalated as he fought for desegregation of public facilities and institutions during the 1940s and 1950s. His work with Justice Thurgood Marshall paved the way for a Supreme Court decision to allow admittance of a black woman, Ada Lois Sipuel, to the University of Oklahoma law school in 1949. Even then, she was required to sit alone in class in a chair marked "colored." She ate in a section of the cafeteria cordoned off by a chain so she could not mix with white students.

Watts fought hard within Oklahoma to ensure that blacks received equal educational opportunities through segregation in the public school system. His efforts benefited his nephew Julius Caesar Watts, who was educated in the newly integrated schools in Eufaula. J. C., as he was known, became a national-class quarterback for the University of Oklahoma, and he was free to saunter the campus unencumbered by racial boundaries.

In 1965, Wade Watts marched with his good friend Martin Luther King Jr. in Selma, Alabama, to demonstrate for racial freedom, justice, and equality. President Lyndon Johnson appointed Watts to the Civil Rights Commission. Within his home state, he served on the Human Rights Commission while maintaining his day job as labor inspector for the Oklahoma State Labor Commission. His passion for racial acceptance started at an early age—after his first exposure to hate.

As a young boy, Wade played with a white companion who invited him home for lunch. He was not allowed to sit at the table; instead, he was led to the back porch, where the mother handed him a bowl of food. The family dog became incensed with Wade, barking and trying to bite him. His friend explained that the dog was mad because Wade was eating out of his dish. This would not be the last time a plate of food reminded him of racial discrimination.

In the late 1950s, Watts and his good friend, the powerful Oklahoma State Senator Gene Stipe, entered an Ada cafe for lunch. The waitress stopped them, saying, "We don't serve Negroes." Watts responded, "I don't eat Negroes. I just came to get some ham and eggs." Leaving the establishment, Stipes asked Watts: If God would grant you one wish, what would it be? The senator anticipated his companion might answer no more hate in the world. Without hesitation, Watts said he wanted to meet the leader of the Ku Klux Klan.

In a small San Francisco suburb, during this time, Johnny Lee Clary was born into a hate-mongering environment. Soon after his birth, the Clary family returned to their small, central Oklahoma hometown of Del City—a predominately white city. His bigoted daddy continued his hard-working ways, while his alcoholic mother strayed with multiple lovers. Johnny Lee's dad, also, taught him those were not "chocolate-covered" men but "niggers." Clary's uncle, Harold, bragged he shot a black man for crossing his yard and only got fined for firing a gun within the city limits.

At age 11, Johnny walked into the house and witnessed his father's suicide. Just as Johnny screamed, "Don't do it," Dad put a .45-caliber slug into his head. Mom quickly moved in with her boyfriend, who beat the traumatized youngster, which prompted Johnny to complain to the police. After law enforcement threatened the couple with jail, the boyfriend delivered an ultimatum: Johnny or him. His mother kicked young Clary out of the house. The tough kid ended up with an older sister in gang-laden Los Angeles, where the beatings continued at the hand of her lover. A despondent Johnny Lee Clary desperately wanted a family that wanted him.

Watching TV one afternoon, Clary found it. The interviewer was questioning David Duke, the Imperial Wizard of the Ku Klux Klan. Recalling Uncle Harold's story, Clary contacted the Klan. An emissary of Duke knocked on his door several weeks later.

The KKK recruiter told him the Klan was a family with a spiritual basis and took him to weekly meetings where people who wanted to hear what he had to say surrounded the teenager. He diligently studied the Klan. He trembled with excitement the day he was officially inducted. Clary was 14. With his new support system's guidance, he had learned how to hate.

Clary ascended the Klan ranks quickly. He went from David Duke's bodyguard to an overly ambitious Kleagle (or recruiter) in Del City to the

Steve Gerkin

leader of the Oklahoma Klan as the Grand Dragon at the not-so-tender age of 21. Clary was on the career path he desired—to become Imperial Wizard of the KKK. His physicality would bring him other successes.[1]

In 1979, an Oklahoma City radio host invited Clary to participate in an on-air debate with a black man. Licking his chops at "a chance to put a black man in his place," Grand Dragon Clary jumped at the chance to spread the gospel of hate. Clary told all his buddies to tune in. His debate opponent was the Reverend Wade Watts, veteran pastor of the Jerusalem Baptist Church in McAlester, Oklahoma.

As the two approached each other for the 1979 broadcast, Clary was shocked.

"He caught me off guard," Clary told an Australian TV host. "I'm expecting this black militant to come in with a great big afro this big (gestures), and an African dashiki on, with bones around and a button on that says 'I hate honkies' and 'Death to crackers.' " But, what he saw was a well-groomed man in a suit and tie, carrying a Bible.

Watts put out his hand and the confused Clary took it, only to withdraw it quickly after the first touch. He had just broken a cardinal Klan rule. The Reverend saw Clary looking at his hand and reassured him, "Don't worry, Johnny. It won't come off."

Clary started calling him a string of epithets.

"I just want to tell you I love you and Jesus loves you," Watts replied.

The on-air back and forth featured Clary spouting off about how the races should not interact, while the reverend calmly quoted scripture. Clary was reduced to mumbling generic Klan slogans.

"I'm not listening to any more," Clary snarled, storming out.

Holding a baby in his arms, the Reverend approached the Grand Dragon, who was hurriedly gathering up his belongings in the lobby. Wade introduced his 14th child, an adopted baby girl, born to a young white girl and black teenage boy.

---

1. While he was the Grand Dragon of Oklahoma, Clary became a professional wrestler. He called himself "Johnny Angel" and won the Arkansas Heavyweight title several times in the late 1980s. His final pro match was a win in Grove, Oklahoma, during a 10-Man Battle Royal in 1988. Still, the Klan was his oyster.

"Mr. Clary, this is my daughter, Tia." As he held out the little girl with shining black eyes and skin, showering Johnny Lee with a sweet smile, Watts said, "You say you hate all black people. Just tell me, how can you hate this child?"

The Dragon nearly ran for the door. Watt's final words rang out like church bells: "God bless you, Johnny. You can't do enough to me to make me hate you. I'm gonna love you and I'm gonna pray for you, whether you like it or not."

The embarrassment caused Clary to turn up the heat on Watts. But intimidating phone calls, crosses burning at his home, and garbage strewn in his front yard failed to curb Watts' public quest for equality.

The Reverend joined up with politicians to outlaw the Klan's racist telemarketing hotlines that recruited for the Klan: "Save the land, join the Klan." Johnny Lee was incensed.

Sporting KKK t-shirts, 30 Klansmen, led by Clary, followed Watts into a McAlester lunch spot. Surrounding him and his plate of fried chicken, Clary chortled, "Hey, boy, I'm gonna make you a promise. We are going to do the same thing to you that you do to that chicken."

Watts surveyed the Klan before picking up a piece of chicken and kissing it. The room erupted with laughter, but Clary was livid.

Clary's robed friends set fire to the Jerusalem Baptist Church. The fire was extinguished before building was destroyed, but Clary felt like gloating, so he called Wade, using a disguised voice. Watts greeted him cordially, saying, "Well, hello, Johnny." He continued, "A man like you takes the time to call me. Let me do something for you." He begins to pray, "Dear Lord, please, forgive Johnny for being so stupid." Then he invited all of them to dinner at Pete's Place in Krebs.

The Klan decided to leave him alone.

For more than a decade, Clary lived in Tulsa near 71st and Lewis. He was a drinker, a fighter, and a womanizer; yet, he never forgot the image of little Tia, and he never forgot the impact of his grandma in Del City praying constantly for him to quit the Klan and find the Lord. He admired Jimmy Swaggart and would smoke cigarettes while listening to Brother Swaggart go on and on about forgiveness. And Tia, who was the illegitimate daughter of a teenage J.C. Watts, sneaked into his consciousness regularly.

STEVE GERKIN

In 1989, Johnny Lee had reached his Klan goal. He became the Imperial Wizard of the White Knights of the Ku Klux Klan—the hate and white supremacy leaders of the world. Yet, there were serious divisions with the Klan. The feds trailed his every move. His girlfriend was unveiled as an FBI informant and the Klan pulled guns on Clary claiming he was untrustworthy. Clary pointed his gun at them and backed out of the room.

The Klan was not the family he thought it might be; rather, it was full of internal hate and mistrust. Like his father before him, Clary picked up his gun, intending to end his life. A ray of sun shone through the blinds and onto his Bible. Setting his gun down, he opened the holy book and read for hours.

Imperial Wizard Johnny Lee Clary quit the Klan after six months of failure. His effort to unite all the hate groups—skinheads, neo-Nazis, Aryan Nation—as a common entity ended in FBI phone tapping, arrests, and brothers of hate turning on each other. He burned his robe in the backyard, feeling that "1,000 pounds" had been removed from his shoulders. He joined Billy Joe Daugherty's Victory Christian Church across from Oral Roberts University and steadfastly immersed himself in Christian education. After two years, he called Reverend Watts.

Clary told him that he had a calling to preach, and Watts invited him to give his first sermon at his rebuilt church. Half of the congregation boycotted his service. When Johnny Lee made the altar call for anyone wanting to turn their life over to Jesus, a 14-year-old black girl came running down the aisle. More followed. As Johnny and the young girl passed Reverend Watts, there were tears staining the elder's face.

"Johnny, you are leading Tia to the Lord," Wade whispered. Three other Watts children joined them at the altar. The former Imperial Wizard brought the last of Watt's 14 children into the house of the Lord.

Watts and Clary became evangelical preachers that drove across the country together. Driving through Arkansas, Clary turned to Watts and asked if he ever thought the two of them would be driving in the same car on their way to save some souls. Wade looked at him, and quipped quickly, "I figured if we were ever in the same car together, you would have me in the trunk." But their relationship was on borrowed time.

Reverend Wade Watts passed in 1998. He is buried in McIntosh County, Oklahoma, beneath his tombstone that reads, "I'd give up silver and gold to have it said that I helped someone."

The Reverend Johnny Lee Clary is with the World Evangelism Fellowship and preaches for Jimmy Swaggart Ministries in Baton Rouge, Louisiana, where he often reminds his international TV audience that Wade Watts preached, "If you want to make beautiful music, you got to use those black and white keys together."

In the end, they enjoyed seven good years of harmony.

TERROR'S LEGACY

Bill Hale became the King of the Osage Hills by marrying
into—and then murdering—a wealthy Osage Indian family

By *Jason Christian*

MARK FREEMAN JR. WAS JUST ACROSS THE KANSAS LINE from
his 3,500-acre cattle ranch. It was in the early 1950s when he and a fellow
rancher were bidding on livestock. His buddy nudged him.

"Look down there, you'll be interested in this," the friend said.

Mark brushed him off. "Son, I'm buying cows."

"You see that man talking to that old cowboy?"

Mark said yes.

"That's Bill Hale."

They both stood and marveled at the man who was never again
supposed to see the light of day.

"His hair was still black. He was dressed in a suit and had a tie—that
son of a bitch always dressed that way." Mark laughed. "I got a kick out
of it because I was raised on them Bill Hale stories."

Now 93, Mark lived through the aftermath of the tragedies known
in Osage County as the Reign of Terror. He was born in 1920 to a white
father (offensively called a "squaw man" in those days) and an Osage
mother. He served as a Tribal Council member and as a member of the
Osage Congress. As a World War II veteran and lifelong rancher, Freeman is a paradigm of the tough-as-nails, no-nonsense cowboy—a Clint
Eastwood type. He didn't have many good things to say about Bill Hale.

"If he'd have come up on someone like I am," he assumed a serious posture, "or I *was* when I was 25 years old—I'd have killed the son of a bitch. Because he was killing my people."

William K. Hale, known as Bill, was a local legend even before he made the papers. He was born and raised in Greenville, Texas, and moved to Osage County around the turn of the 20th century. It was a time when cattlemen and roughnecks were coming in droves to make it rich, or just to make it at all. Freeman says that Hale "started out in a tent," alone and ambitious, before he sent for his wife and nephews to join him on the Oklahoma prairie.

If his humble roots didn't win people over, his showmanship helped. Hale could entertain crowds with the best of them. He told jokes, did rope tricks, and handled a horse like an expert. And then there was his famous gift giving. He liked to cheer the kids up by buying them ponies, and won over townsfolk with brand-new suits. He co-signed loans and visited the sick and elderly. I was told that he brought loads of beef and pork to the yearly Osage dances. I imagine him as a sort of people's aristocrat, a saintly cowboy gentleman. He even gained a position as reserve deputy sheriff. He was the kind of outsider the locals admired: A self-made man who was everyone's friend.

In time, Hale's wealth caught up to his personality. He owned a couple of homes, one in Fairfax and a ranch house in the country. He owned 5,000 acres of grazing land and leased another 45,000 more from Osage landowners. He invested in a bank, a general store, and a funeral home. With so much wealth[1] and influence, he started calling himself "King of the Osage Hills." And he started to act like it.

HEADRIGHTS AND GUARDIANS

When Hale arrived to Osage County, the Osage tribe was not yet wealthy. That story is a marvel on its own. A unique economic arrangement was set up for the Osage. Back in 1906, when the tribe was forced to divide the allotments of its communally owned land, they gave every

---

1. The *New York Times* reported in 1926 that he was worth half a million dollars ($75 million today).

member—all 2,229 of them—an equal share of land and mineral rights brought in by the tribe. Even as the tribe grew in numbers there would forever be just 2,229 equal shares from then on. Some of the money came from grassland leases, but the vast majority came from the seemingly bottomless lakes of oil beneath Osage County. The royalty payments from mineral income became known as "headrights." Headright payments began modest but soon everyone was surprised at their incredible gains. The Osage became wealthy seemingly overnight. They built mansions and hired butlers, bought luxury automobiles and hired chauffeurs. But their opulence didn't sit well with the racist and jealous of America. Apparently, even some newspapers felt the tribe didn't deserve their newfound wealth.

Because the Osage seemed to be blowing all their money, at least to the passive observer 1,200 miles away in Washington, D.C., action was taken. Congress passed a law in 1921 requiring all[2] Osages of one-half blood quantum or higher to have a "guardian." The guardians (pronounced *gar-deen* locally) were there to give Osages their royalty checks every quarter and help them spend it "wisely." But guardians were only required to pay Osages (under guardianship) $1,000 a quarter, even when headright earnings were three times higher.[3] With little to no oversight, the rest just seemed to evaporate, and almost immediately Osages under guardianship began dying.

"These damn lawyers, and some damn preachers—not all preachers are good—would be guardians for three, four, five people," Mark Freeman Jr. told me.

THE MURDERS

The first murder shocked the public, but Hale wasn't yet a suspect.

In 1921 a young full-blood Osage woman named Anna Kyle Brown was found dead in a ravine with a gunshot wound to her head. The local undertaker and two doctors conducted a crude autopsy on Brown,

---

2. If Osages could prove they were "competent" to an unsympathetic court, they could get out of having a guardian. Many gave up or didn't try.
3. In 1923, the peak earnings for every headright shareholder was $11,800.

hacking up her body and quickly disposing of it. The tribe was horrified, and many wondered about the integrity of the doctors.

An inquest was held and revealed little. One of the last men to see Anna alive was a man named Byron Burkhart, Bill Hale's nephew. He was questioned and denied any wrongdoing. Authorities had nothing on him and released him, and the whole matter was dropped. Life went on.

More murders followed. Anna Brown's cousin Henry Roan was found shot to death. William Stepson, a rodeo star, died in his bed, allegedly of poison. Charles Whitehorn, Joe Yellow Horse, Henry Benet, Hugh Gibson—the list is long, and to this day the number of murders is debated. Nevertheless, Osage County remained relatively quiet—until the explosion.

On March 10, 1923, a house in Fairfax was obliterated by a bomb, sending debris into the trees and yards all over town. A white man, W.E. "Bill" Smith, and his Osage wife, Reta née Kyle (Anna's sister), owned the home. Reta and their housekeeper, Nettie Brookshire, were killed instantly from the blast. Bill died a few days later, taking to the grave anything he might have known about his wife's family's murders.

Something had to be done. The Osage Tribal Council desperately appealed to the federal government for help.[4] Within weeks the newly formed Federal Bureau of Investigation launched a major investigation in which they pioneered the use of undercover agents and informants.

When the feds arrived to Pawhuska, they discovered a complicated mess, and the agents were not welcomed. FBI files say that they found Osage County to be dangerous and full of uncooperative "transient 'potlickers' [sic], oil workers, poor whites." An atmosphere of fear permeated the area; however, they began to piece together many of the crimes against the Osage people that were happening right under the nose of law enforcement. A conspiracy was unfolding that would have made its murdering mastermind wealthy beyond anyone's imagination. A whole Osage family was being targeted, it appeared. Anna Kyle Brown had been the first.[5] Her mother, Lizzie, died soon after (maybe from natural causes, maybe not), and then Anna's cousin Henry Roan (on whom Hale had taken out a $25,000 life insurance policy and later sued to collect). The next in line to die were

---

4. The price the FBI took for their services amounted to $20,000.
5. Anna Kyle Brown was pregnant when she was murdered and it was widely believed that Bill Hale was the father.

TERROR'S LEGACY

the Smiths and their unfortunate servant. And the last heir, Mollie Kyle, happened to be married to Earnest Burkhart, Bill Hale's other nephew.

With the benefit of hindsight, the plan looks simple and obvious: As each member of the Kyle family was killed, his or her headright would pass to the next of kin. Each death would bring all of the headrights closer to Burkhart's hands, who would either share his spoils with Hale, or else he would surely be eliminated. But still no one had implicated Hale.

Yet more deaths occurred. Like George Bigheart, son of the last hereditary chief of the Osage tribe. And attorney William Vaughn, who was purported to be investigating the recent murders. Bigheart died in his bed, from an unidentified illness. Vaughn, after visiting Bigheart in the hospital, was conveniently thrown off a moving train as he was returning to Pawhuska. These murders happened three months *after* the FBI began their investigation.

The feds moved sluggishly. Death after mysterious death was marked down as natural or accidental. Autopsies were rare and investigations even more so. Finally, after deaths had reached apocalyptic levels, the FBI and Bureau of Indian Affairs had enough evidence to make arrests. Bill Hale and a few members of his gang—besides the ones who mysteriously died around that time[6]—stood on trial for murder.

A long battle of jurisdiction between state and federal courts ensued. After wading through tampered juries, bribed or threatened witnesses, perjured and falsified testimonies, and several grueling trials, justice finally prevailed—kind of. William Hale and a hired gunman got life sentences, though they were paroled after just 20 years.[7] Hale's nephew Earnest Burkhart only served 11 years and was inexplicably pardoned by Governor Henry Bellmon, and everyone else either got a slap on the

---

6. The most well-known of them was Henry Grammar, a world-champion roper turned bootlegger and criminal. He died mysteriously in a car accident shortly after the FBI began their investigations. Many suspect he was killed by Bill Hale.

7. Hale was known to consort with organized crime bosses from Kansas City ("thieves and bounders," according to Mark Freeman Jr.), and Mark also believes that his eventual parole came from an underhanded relationship with President Harry Truman, of Kansas City.

8. Kelsey Morrison received a life sentence for Anna Brown's murder but was paroled after just a few years. He was later involved in other crimes and was killed in a shootout with the police in 1937. - See more at: http://thisland-press.com/08/14/2013/terrors-legacy/?read=complete#f5

wrist or walked free.[8] The sensational case made national headlines; the FBI website has more than 3,200 pages dedicated to it. Reading like bad noir, the FBI describes the details of Hale's plan and the Bureau's success in thwarting it. The Bureau considered the Hale case a triumph of justice, even as corpses were surfacing during and after the trials.

"The FBI, once Bill Hale was convicted, dropped the whole case. Didn't go on any further," Mary Jo Webb, a retired teacher, told me. "There were many murders that weren't taken up by the government." And she went on to tell me about her own grandfather's controversial death after the Hale conviction. A full-blood, one of the original allottees with a full headright, Webb's grandfather was killed in a hit and run accident, resulting in a third of his headright landing in the lap of his former wife, a white woman.

"History's going to remove all the full-bloods," Webb said. "That's the modern day history of how the Osages have been decimated by greed. There's a lot more stories that never made the paper."

The FBI tallied at least two dozen murders. Others claim hundreds of Osages were killed, if one looks back before the 1920s. Webb admits, "It's a long story. It would take days." There is no way of calculating the damage done to her people, she says.

Webb, a former member of the Osage Constitutional Commission, has been trying to bring these facts to light all her life. At 79, she has a reputation as Fairfax's expert on the Reign of Terror.

"They [the killings] were labeled as 'accidents.' Or they were poisoned and they said, 'He had a bad stomach.' " Some Osages were drugged or whiskey-ed, only to find themselves married to a swindler the next day.

Even now, Webb told me, there are white descendants who have inherited "a piece of some full-blood's estate [and] they think, 'I'm probably part Osage, or I'm close to this family.' Of course, that's just not true." People don't know the history, and that is part of the problem, she says. "I made sure my family knew who was responsible [for my grandfather's death]."

---

8. Kelsey Morrison received a life sentence for Anna Brown's murder but was paroled after just a few years. He was later involved in other crimes and was killed in a shootout with the police in 1937. - See more at: http://thisland-press.com/08/14/2013/terrors-legacy/?read=complete#f5

TERROR'S LEGACY

Mary Jo Webb pulled out a box of files (she had two more in the other room) and began showing me newspaper clippings, photographs, and other material on the subject. She had a reputation for doing independent research, but nothing ever materialized into a book. However, she did put together an exposé on some of the killings and some of those responsible who never went to jail. Around 20 years ago, she placed the document in the Fairfax library and it eventually went missing. Not long after that she received an anonymous phone call from a man threatening to kill her. I asked her why someone would give her anonymous death threats and she replied candidly, "I named names."

In Osage County today, you see a few elegant buildings boarded up and a few mansions in shambles. The only indicators of an oil economy that I saw were some scattered derricks in the wide open prairie that was once forested them, and a company on the edge of Pawhuska selling oil field parts and used pump jacks. Signs of a legacy of murders are less tangible. The old-timers know it in their bones. And the younger ones seem to be just trying to get by and move on from the haunting past that traumatized their elders nearly a century ago.

DOGS PLAYING POKER

On Oklahoma's last duel and the myth of moral progress

By *Brian Ted Jones*

A FINE OCTOBER SATURDAY IN 1966, in Fort Gibson, Oklahoma. A residential neighborhood within this community of a thousand souls. Peace and quiet. Folks chatting, dogs barking, kids flying by on bicycles. A 48-year-old man named Pete McLemore says goodbye to his wife, Goldie, and leaves the house. He's headed for work; he's a security guard at the local glass factory. McLemore's also the Fort Gibson treasurer, and has been for 16 years. He's a well-known figure. He waves at friends as he heads down the driveway to his car.

A pickup truck rolls down the street, but McLemore doesn't see it, his view obstructed by a nearby magnolia tree. Inside the truck are two men. The passenger is Bill Bennett, the Fort Gibson mayor. The driver is Johnny Scott, the town's 32-year-old marshal.

Johnny exits the truck with a 9mm pistol taped to a rifle stock. A few witnesses would later say Johnny also held a piece of paper in his hand—a warrant, perhaps, for McLemore's arrest.

Others say he just started firing.

McLemore, a World War II veteran, hears the shots. Something happens in his heart, something bad, but he doesn't have time to think about that. He darts for his car, bullets flying all around him. He kneels by the driver's side door, fumbling for the latch. He keeps a 12 gauge automatic shotgun in the vehicle, so it's there when he needs it. He needs it now.

But not because Johnny Scott was any great shakes as a gunfighter. In fact, in spite of his job in law enforcement, Scott displayed zero talent as a marksman. McLemore would later say that he was "just spraying all around."

"He shot about 20–25 times at me. I don't know how he kept from hitting me."

But that's how it went. Pete McLemore—huddled, scared, caught wildly off-guard, and subjected to heavy fire—didn't suffer a scratch. Johnny Scott was nowhere near that lucky. McLemore nailed his young assailant three times—in the chest, the arm, and the leg. In fact, maybe Scott *was* lucky, in that McLemore—excellent shot that he was, even under stress—*wasn't* shooting to kill.

"I never shot at his head," McLemore would say. "I shot for the bulk of him."

And where was Mayor Bennett in all that haze? We don't know. McLemore thought he saw three other shots come at him from a separate attacker, but that's likely just battle fog. Witnesses clearly observed the gunfight between Scott and McLemore, but didn't identify any other participants.

The cops, though, found Bennett carrying guns away from the scene. They arrested him on the spot, along with Pete McLemore. They'd have certainly arrested Johnny Scott, too, had he not already been in an ambulance, gunning for Muskogee General.

McLemore soon joined him. At the county jail, deputies discovered that all the excitement had given the poor man a heart attack.

Five days later, Muskogee District Attorney Paul Ferguson announced a set of charges related to the shoot-out. They raised a few eyebrows. McLemore and Scott were both charged with "dueling and agreeing to a duel." Bennett was charged as an accessory. Ferguson also charged McLemore with shooting with intent to kill. It was the first time in 42 years anyone in Oklahoma had faced prosecution under the 1910 anti-dueling statute.

Even as he encountered surprise and amusement from the press, Ferguson defended his position. He explained that the law allowed a prosecution for dueling to stem from "threatening words or even mere implications of violence."

Pete McLemore thought little of the accusation.

"There was no damn duel," he said. "It was a planned attempt on my life."

The U.S. Constitution was just 16 years old when the republic's third vice president killed its first secretary of the treasury. In true gangster fashion, Aaron Burr shot Alexander Hamilton in the belly. POTUS number 7, "Old Hickory" Andrew Jackson, was a renowned duelist, wounded so often he was said to "rattle like a sack of marbles." He's the only president (we know of) to have actually killed another man in a duel. Thomas Hart "Old Bullion" Benton (not the painter; rather, the first senator from Missouri) killed a rival named Charles Lucas in a duel on Bloody Island, on the Mississippi River near St. Louis.

American naval commander Stephen Decatur died in a duel—betrayed by his second, Commodore William Bainbridge, who had always been jealous of the younger, more famous Decatur, and arranged the duel's set-up to maximize the odds of each participant's death.

Speaker of the House (and later senator) Henry Clay fought a duel with John Randolph, who at various times had served as congressman, senator and ambassador to Russia. Two sitting representatives, William J. Graves of Kentucky and Jonathan Cilley of Maine, fought a duel in Washington, D.C., actually while on break from their legislative duties. This gunfight prompted Congress to pass a law making it illegal to issue or accept a duel challenge within the nation's capital.

Senator Gwin and Congressman McCorkle dueled in 1853; Senator Broderick and former Chief Justice of the Supreme Court of California David S. Terry dueled in 1859. Even Abraham Lincoln, who is generally considered something of a sweetheart, got mixed up in dueling way back in 1842. Fortunately, some friends intervened to call off the affair. In the ranks of American political history, perhaps only adulterers are better represented than duelists.

There's a flipside to Socrates' notion that those who least desire power are best equipped to wield it: Those who most desire power will most

BRIAN TED JONES

reliably behave like perfect beasts once they get it. These sorts of men do not take insults lightly. Like the princess in the story of the pea, they can sense the tiniest imperfections in the way others regard them. And like most dynamic men, they are built with short fuses.

Take the Fort Gibson matter, which all started in January 1966 when the Fort Gibson Utility Authority sent Pete McLemore his regular water bill, but with an unwelcome addition: a $6.60 tab for "sewer services." McLemore contested the charge (he had his own septic tank); but the authorities said he had to pay up or get his water shut off.

This sat uneasily with McLemore—he'd fought for his country in a war, he'd worked hard all his life, and he didn't appreciate the government making him pay for something he hadn't bought and didn't need.

He also knew how to juke the system. He let the municipality go ahead and shut off his water (making up the difference by tapping a nearby well), then led the town fathers down a series of legal rabbit holes—lawsuits and writs of mandamus—which challenged the very basis of the Utility Authority's right to exist.

Right after McLemore went to court, Bennett called for a town meeting—of all Fort Gibson's 1,000 residents—for no other purpose than to discuss the Pete McLemore issue.

That is some weapons-grade orneriness, on both men's parts. We don't know what slights and insults had passed between these two in the years before 1966. But as the American newspaperman Jacob Riis would point out, it is not the final strike from the stonecutter that splits the rock in two, but all that came before it.

Legal wrangling notwithstanding, the courts ordered McLemore to pay the bill. One judge helpfully suggested he pay it "under protest," so he could stay out of trouble and still wage his crusade. McLemore wasn't trying to hear any of that. He was prepared to see the inside of a jail cell over this business.

And he did. On June 9, 1966, Fort Gibson Marshal Johnny Scott arrested Pete McLemore for not paying the sewer bill. McLemore bonded out quickly, but it wasn't the last time that summer he'd be jailed over his protest. And always, it was Johnny Scott slapping on the handcuffs.

DOGS PLAYING POKER

Unlike McLemore and Bennett, Scott was a newcomer to Fort Gibson politics, having first been elected to his post in 1965. If McLemore was your grumpy old Tea Party grandpa, Scott was your right-wing brother-in-law, the guy who bitches loudly during Thanksgiving dinner about government handouts while Medicaid pays health insurance for all the children he's fathered. One paper described Scott as a "235-pound former blacksmith," and he apparently liked to throw his weight around. Another newspaper report speaks of violent threats and even incidents of "gun-waving" between the two enemies. Scott also managed, by late August of that year, to get actual human blood on his hands.

That blood came from Buster Vann, a 71-year-old black man whom the papers described as a "Fort Gibson welfare recipient." He died of a cerebral hemorrhage after Johnny Scott bashed him over the head with a blackjack—three times—while trying to arrest him for public intoxication.

In response to this killing, District Attorney Ferguson charged Scott with manslaughter. A lesser man might have decided he was in enough trouble at that point, but not Johnny Scott. A month later and he's sneaking up on Pete McLemore's house in broad daylight.

For every Aaron Burr ruined by success in dueling; for every "Old Hickory" rendered highest honors in spite of his prowess at organized murder; for all the men whose spots in history are assured, regardless of any reputational damage suffered from dueling; and for all the men who could have been anything—president, speaker, chief justice, or general— had not a snarl of vanity earned them a heart full of lead. There must be unthinkable numbers of aldermen, burgesses, sheriffs, and county commissioners whose own small-time *affaires d'honneur* either barred, or did not bar, their political advancement.

That's the thing about dueling, as with adultery: It either matters, or it doesn't. A politician can survive it, or he can't. As Americans, we tend to retain certain rigid ideas of what's allowable in our officials, and what's disqualifying—while indulging them anything, so long as it's not weird or out of character. Before Clinton, no adultery. Before Bush, no DUIs. Before Obama, no drug use. We forgive these men because their sins are human and appropriate to the times. Such failings may even have political advantages: We see our flaws in their flaws and we sympathize.

What we won't allow, though, is outlandishness. District Attorney Ferguson dusted off the anti-dueling statute when the police reports hit his desk, probably because he honestly thought that law best covered the situation as presented. In the end, though, he decided to drop it—likely a wise choice.

As for the men who faced those charges, Mayor Bennett quickly snaked out of his trouble. McLemore, whose health deteriorated rapidly after the shooting, was clearly dealt some form of prosecutorial mercy—his charges for shooting Johnny Scott went away completely. Even Scott walked, though he would eventually be convicted for the death of Buster Vann. For that crime, he received a 4-year prison sentence, which he was able to overturn on appeal because of procedural hiccups at trial. But his career in Fort Gibson politics was over.

So was Pete McLemore's. He quit as treasurer, claiming he feared Scott or Bennett would try to kill him if he set foot in City Hall. Instead, his wife, Goldie, ran in his place, and ultimately tied votes with her opponent. She won a coin toss to succeed her husband, but would die a few years later in 1973. Pete held on only five years longer.

Scott likely died in 2000: an obituary for one "Johnny Scott" ran in the *Sequoyah County Times* on January 20 of that year. His age at death was listed as 65; the math works out exactly. Strangely, the obituary also contains this sentence: "He was sheriff of Muskogee County during the early 1960s."

That's a flatly incorrect. The sheriff of Muskogee County from 1958 to 1990 was a man named Bill Vinzant. He was actually a responding officer the day of the shoot-out. He may even have been the one to put Johnny Scott in that ambulance.

We Americans are a tribe of stunning contradictions. The greatest force for peace and justice the world has ever known; but our country is a crime scene, our wealth built on a holocaust of Indian slaughter and African slavery, and we alone have used the atomic bomb against our fellow human beings. We present interesting proof of La Rochefoucauld's claim that hypocrisy is an homage vice pays to virtue. Just look at the governor's

Dogs Playing Poker

oath in the Kentucky, which to this day requires an incoming official to swear he has never taken part in any mortal duel; but the very rules of American dueling were written and promulgated by another governor, John Lyde Wilson of South Carolina.

We might flatter ourselves that we've turned some corner in human evolution, that we're beyond the growl of primitive impulses, that we've outgrown those creaky old procedures of violence. We think on our blood-soaked, dueling past, and those men with their pistols and rapiers, counting off steps and deputizing seconds, appear to us like dogs playing poker—ludicrously bound up in protocols and conventions, while the naked animal truth shines clear, in all its fullness of absurdity.

We've outgrown nothing. On September 11, 2012, the BBC reported that a man named Gediminas Stauskas of Drumgrannon Road in Northern Ireland admitted to killing Audrius Aukstuolis. The men were both Lithuanians. Stauskas received a five-and-a-half-year prison sentence for the killing.

Aukstuolis had pursued Stauskas's girlfriend. Stauskas threatened to kill Aukstuolis over the issue. They agreed to meet and settle their dispute. They got together in a parking lot. Each man brought a weapon: Stauskas a knife, Aukstuolis a screwdriver.

They apparently arranged the whole thing using text messages.

HOME ON THE RANGE

Going great guns in the land of concealed—and
now open—carry

BY *Natasha Ball*

MY HUSBAND AND I PULLED INTO THE PARKING LOT of the
United States Shooting Academy early in the morning, taking a driveway
that seemed like a wrong turn, just beyond the Tulsa Police Academy.
Aaron had packed everything we'd need for the day and nothing
more: hats, ammunition, pistol, holster, spare magazine, magazine
pouch, aluminum bottles of water. He packed us a pair of identical
lunches: some slices of leftover ham and carrot sticks in Ziploc bags.
We intended to satisfy the qualification requirements to legally carry
firearms, concealed on our person—or, as we heard we would be able
to do starting in late fall, carried openly on a hip—for lawful self-
defense. In our state, under the Oklahoma Self-Defense Act, that meant
a morning in a classroom with a few dozen people we had never met,
all of them armed. It was something we could do together. A day date.

My husband is the gun enthusiast, the kind who loves to shoot
but can't watch war movies anymore. He was the Army specialist with
coffee eyes who stared back at me from a photo, snapped while he was
on patrol just outside his basecamp east of Kabul. Between him and
a gray sky were trees growing out of an open pit. Hanging from his
shoulder were an M4 carbine and an M203 grenade launcher, barrels
pointed to the dust, the guns held flat against his torso in presentation,

NATASHA BALL

more by default than with pride. Peeking out from far behind him was a boy, one of the many children who followed when the soldiers circled the camp, pelting the armed men with tiny rocks when they refused to surrender their pencils and candy. The photo troubled me, but I'd sneak moments at work to open it, to search for new things to notice about it. I liked the look of Aaron's right hand, how his palm relaxed around the shape of the pistol grip, the casual way he held his index finger just a breath from the trigger. I thought about the boy in the background. He was hiding from the camera, behind the man with the big gun.

Aaron is an expert marksman, a product of the U.S. Army's sniper school in Fort Benning, where the country's elite fire bullets through the boughs of Georgia pines. From his weekend drills he would bring home pennies with holes like exploded blisters, which he'd shot from a distance longer than the height of the Golden Driller, about 80 feet, using iron sights. Proud, he put one of the pennies above our fireplace, where we kept our family photos. But I had decided to ignore the rifles in our closet and the revolvers in our bedside table. Only people who favored the death penalty and voted for Bush 43 collected guns. Besides, they had failed to keep my husband safe from the nightmares, which then were just starting, intruders in the night that attacked while the guns slept. But his only trophies in life had been for pulling triggers. He convinced me to go with him to a nearby gun club, where for the first time I watched him flatten his belly to the grass, gold and dry with winter, and nest the rifle he kept in our closet in the hollow of his arm. They lay there, the two of them, for what seemed like too long, the rise and fall of Aaron's breath hidden underneath his coat. They were hundreds of yards from their target, but not far enough away from me to know that they'd gone elsewhere together, to the hidden place animals go when they're charmed by a target. More minutes passed. When he finally fired the shot, the sound reacted with the sky, blooming and expanding as it rose. But his body hadn't as much as flinched. The sound of the bullet as it pierced the metal target made its way back to us, singing like the rim of a spittoon. My husband and a rifle had outsmarted the Oklahoma wind that blew across the range. After a few rounds at the handgun range, we went for a lunch of fried fish planks, served stacked in plastic baskets atop beds of leftover batter. I sat in the chair at his side rather than the one opposite, and we sipped

HOME ON THE RANGE

from a shared root beer. He sat with his elbows on the table, eating hushpuppies with hands trained to kill.

We had been told to report at quarter to eight, to a windowless classroom inside the main building at USSA, more a hunting lodge than a training facility. At home, I dragged getting dressed. I knew I wasn't going to get the license. I couldn't see myself at work, at the grocery store, in the car on the way to pick up our four-year-old from preschool, with the telltale outline of a pistol showing through my clothes—me as one of those people. I felt guilty after I signed up for the course, especially since what I was doing as a stunt—at best, out of curiosity—seemed to settle my husband. A new book I ordered had arrived, and I was behind on laundry. But I couldn't forget that a firearm and I were a team on which my husband was willing to bet. As it turned out, the coffee at the academy was decent. Some people recognized me, saying they listened to me on the radio. On our breaks from class my husband and I flashed each other pictures we found in magazines and calendars in the pro shop of girls in camo bikinis wielding assault rifles. We lounged on the black leather couches in the lobby, eating M&M's from the vending machine.

That morning, our teacher—a competition sharpshooter—clicked through the slides of a PowerPoint presentation. John Zane is a veteran, a pastured Army medic with a job as a factory maintenance mechanic. At some point, he completed at least 16 hours of firearms instructor training to qualify to teach the concealed-carry course gig at USSA. The motto embossed into some rubber bracelets we got at registration read, "Win the Fight!" For Zane, the fight is for life. He keeps a copy of the Constitution—its touchy Second Amendment sandwiched between those promising freedoms of religion and speech, and having enemy soldiers sleeping on your sofa—in the front pocket of his camo-print backpack. He hides a handgun in his clothes when he showers at home. He avoids bars, mostly because concealed weapons aren't typically allowed there. Even if they were, Zane told us, he has never drawn a gun on anyone before, and since he'd like to keep it that way, it's best to avoid places like bars. Zane likes to tell his students that there is enough metal inside of his body to build a lawn chair. That's because about a week before Christmas in 2011, a Broken Arrow school bus rolled over him twice and dragged him nearly 200 feet. He was armed the day of the accident, he told us.

Zane has boyish, ornery eyes, like he knows all the best places to reload. During our section on Oklahoma's "Make My Day" law, he played a tape of a 911 call. A gun was the hero, in the right place at the right time, saving a woman from an intruder attempting to break into her home. Moral of the story was, he'd rather hose off the porch than shampoo the carpet. Later Zane showed us, by drawing with a marker on a whiteboard, how, when you shoot someone, you're shooting a fluid-filled sack, ballistically speaking. For those times when you really need to stop someone, like in the case of the woman in the 911 call, to release the maximum amount of energy from the bullet into said sack, see about hollow points, which work like big meat drills, blossoming like a flower and sticking to the insides of a transgressor. Zane spoke of the various options available to women who choose to carry a concealed weapon—there are fewer than those of men, mostly because of how our clothing is cut. My husband put down his pencil when he realized I was taking better notes.

Inside of half an hour, we put 50 rounds into the dirt berms outside, the exact number required by the state to qualify for concealed-carry licensing. When we returned to our classroom, Zane called each of us by name to his desk. He signed two copies of our course-completion certificates—one to walk to the sheriff's office with the license application and one for us to keep, to hang on a wall if we so wished. We got to keep our range targets, too, which sunk to the bottom of my trunk as I drove through the summer. This winter, as we filled the hallway in our house with new picture frames, we joked that we should find a spot for the USSA certificates. Aaron knew exactly where they were. He walked into our office and pulled a crisp manila folder out of a filing cabinet we share. He'd kept our certificates there, together with some of our son's drawings, and other of his precious things.

LOCKER ROOM CONFIDENTIAL

Is football's warrior code of manliness creating a
compassionless subculture?

By *Russell Cobb*

Rob and I watched the scrimmage from the sidelines,
helmets off. We weren't getting any playing time, so why bother paying
attention? I heard the whiz of a football and then a thud as it hit Rob in
the back of the head. Rob flinched like he had been stung by a swarm of
bees. His forearms clasped the sides of his head and he shook, trying to
hold back tears. I turned around and saw John, the senior placekicker—
the kicker!—laughing at us.

"Get your head in the game, frosh!" he said.

Later, after practice, Mike, a vicious pit bull of a linebacker, waved a
silver tablespoon at us freshmen in the locker room. "See this, frosh? It's
going up your ass! Might be today, might be in a week, you never know."
Mike had vacant black eyes and a mouth that hung slightly agape, giving
him the aura of a sociopath in training. He chuckled through his threats.

A trio of seniors led by Mike pinned a freshman—we'll call him
Josh—to a bench. I looked on in horror as one of them waved the
tablespoon in the air while the others struggled to get Josh into position.
An assistant coach walked in before they could get his pants down. In the
presence of a coach, the bullying subsided to innocent teasing. The coach
told us we were all "family." We had to have each other's backs through
two-a-days because we were going to war in class 2A Oklahoma football.

Mike never got the spoon up Josh's ass, but he did manage to cram him into a locker and padlock it from the outside. He was discovered hours later by the baseball coach. This was, of course, all in the name of toughening Josh up, making a man out of him. In fact, it did the opposite. Josh turned into a freakish mess of anxiety, petulance, and rage for the next few years. We had been friends, but even I began to avoid him.

After the tablespoon incident, I went home and told my mom I was quitting football. This was quite a revelation, since I had been a relentless and dedicated defensive end, once labeled a "fucking devastator" by my best friend's father-in-law. My mom took me to see one of the school administrators, a middle-aged priest with a perfect helmet of black hair and thick silver-rimmed glasses. "You never want to be known as a quitter," Father McMurray said. "If you leave the team, that's what you'll be. Is that how you want to go through life—as a quitter?"

"No, Father," I said, staring at the ground. On at least one occasion, Father McMurray had punched a student in the hallway for mocking him.

I thought about the priest's proposition for a while. Go back to Mike and the crew, whose idea of fun was anally assaulting freshmen, or be a quitter for the rest of my life. Even to a confused 15-year-old, it seemed like a false dichotomy. I decided to stick to my decision, but not reveal the real reason why I left the football team. I deflected any questions about it by saying I wanted to focus on basketball, which I played all four years. In fact, I've never mentioned the episode of Mike and the tablespoon publicly until now.

I went to a Catholic school in Oklahoma 20 years ago; my story of powerful males bullying weaker males seems, in this universe, a law of nature or part of the Great Chain of Being.

Some people see the Richie Incognito–Jonathan Martin controversy as a purely NFL scandal. I see it as symptomatic of a subculture (football in general) that has lost touch with the basics of human compassion. Incognito, a veteran guard for the Miami Dolphins, bullied Martin, a second-year tackle, relentlessly, calling him a "half-nigger" and threatening to "shit in [his] fucking mouth." Incognito had a long rap sheet of dirty play (apparently gouging eyes of opposing players) and borderline criminal behavior off the field (he allegedly sexually assaulted a female volunteer with a golf club).

Andrew Sharp of Grantland.com recently wrote about a chasm between mainstream culture and the NFL. "There's a disconnect between people who play professional sports and people who watch them," Sharp wrote, "and that gulf is probably a lot wider than we realize. Even if a world full of all-access shows and instant information allows us to know more about athletes and locker rooms than ever before, we may never actually understand any of this."

Many NFL players themselves think that it's the insular nature of the professional locker room that separates the sport from us mere mortals. Former Dolphins running back Ricky Williams, for example, said: "The NFL, it's really like a closed fraternity. I don't think the media, I don't think fans, I don't think anyone outside is really in a position to really fully understand what occurs inside of a locker room and inside of a football team." When I look at the face of Richie Incognito, though, I see Mike waving that silver tablespoon. When I consider how the Miami Dolphins organization—the coach and the GM—could be so ignorant of the reality of the locker room, I think of our coach insisting we were a "family." When I see Incognito's smirk, I think of Mike and his buds, their disdain for the weak—the eggheads, faggots, the pussies—who can't handle it, who can't man up.

Maybe you've had a Richie Incognito or a Mike in your life: a supervisor who made you redo a meaningless task just because he could; a teacher who humiliated you in front of the class; a co-worker who sent you threatening emails and then claimed it was all a joke. In most walks of life, this sort of behavior isn't tolerated, and it's a matter of time before the bully gets his just desserts.

But in football—and only in football—this sort of behavior is seen as "tough"; it's part of the warrior code of manliness.

Actual warriors, though, have given up on hazing. "Hazing doesn't make you tough," one Marine sergeant said recently. "It makes you stupid." Marines have been court-martialed for hazing, which is strictly forbidden in the Armed Forces. Forty-nine states have laws against bullying and/ or hazing; California even made hazing a felony.

Emily Bazelon's recent book *Sticks and Stones: Defeating the Culture of Bullying and Rediscovering the Power of Character and Empathy* cites statistics showing that high school bullies are much more likely to end up as criminals and addicts than the rest of us. They suffer disproportionately from mental illness. The victims of bullies are prone to suicide and depression. Victims of bullying often repeat the cycle by becoming bullies themselves. Far from toughening up its victims, locker room bullying creates another generation of sociopaths who think the way to improve performance on the field is to scream at and humiliate a young person.

Football is supposedly a "warrior culture," but what war is it fighting? What is the noble cause? Some vague notion of tradition or manliness moored to an atavistic worldview, one the rest of society left behind decades ago? When it's a spectacle on television, it's just another show with violence, athleticism, and ego on full display. But when its realities— brain damage, bullying, mental illness, suicide—come home to roost, how can we go on watching?

Even though I made the decision to quit high school football, the sport pulled me back in for the better part of a year. In 2003, I went to Paris on a teacher exchange program. Not knowing anyone, I started reading an English-language newspaper and discovered a group of Parisians who played American flag football.

Flag football, for me, was a tease. The most seductive thing about football was the full-bore crunch of a hit delivered on a player with a ball cradled in his arm. (I never really cared for offense.) The guy who managed the flag-football league noticed my over-zealous flag-pulling and told me that he might be able to sponsor me to play on his full-contact team—the Corsaires d'Évry.

I showed up a week later and experienced a Proustian moment as the smell of sweaty shoulder pads and the sound of helmets cracking brought back crisp Oklahoma fall days. I forgot about Mike and his tablespoon. All I remembered was the thrill of sprinting down the field in eighth grade and obliterating some kick returner, jarring the ball loose, and then pouncing on it.

I was put under the tutelage of J.P., the defensive coordinator for Corsaires, a semi-pro team that played in France's only American football league. I made the cut as one of only two Americans on the team, but our first road trip brought out the whack jobs. On the way back to Paris from a game in the south of France, one of the rookies was de-pantsed as he slept on the bus. Two guys held him down and another rubbed IcyHot on his testicles. He screamed and, freeing himself from the grips of his tormentors, jumped around the bus, his balls on icy fire.

Most of the team tried to ignore the scene, but the bullies (studies show that it's usually a minority who wields power over the weakest members) laughed and mocked the rookie's pain. I kept my head down, but then one pointed at me. I was to be next on their list. They were going to devise a special torture session for me, *l'américain*.

That's when I quit football for the second time.

OK, OK, some people say. Sure, some of this is a bit harsh, but you turned out fine, right? In the end, can't we laugh at the hijinks as stupid pranks. Wasn't Incognito just joking?

Believe me, I would like to laugh it off. I would like nothing more than to crack open a cold one and plop down on the La-Z-Boy and watch some hittin' on the TV. Come this weekend, I might just do that.

I just can't do so with a clear conscience anymore. Even if football locker rooms suddenly became Oprah book clubs, there's still the mounting evidence that the sport itself is becoming a major public health crisis.[1]

But these guys are paid handsomely to play a sport they love, you say. It's their choice! The nanny state shouldn't be telling grown-ass men what to do with their bodies! Indeed. If I want to go smash heads with someone, that's my right—just as it's my right to smoke cigarettes and risk lung cancer.

Let's think about an uncomfortable truth for a moment, however: Why is the NFL the richest sport in America? Because of the brutal hits, something viewers demand and young players want to imitate. These repeated hits lead to CTE (Chronic Traumatic Encephalopathy), a disease that, in turn, leads to depression, rage, suicide, and/or dementia.

The growing list of players diagnosed with CTE symptoms now includes college and high school players, not just NFL veterans. There's a legitimate

---

1. For a primer on the crisis, see the Frontline/PBS documentary *League of Denial.*

debate whether CTE is directly caused by football concussions, or whether there's a combination of hits, bad genes, and/or other lifestyle issues, but the booming number of football players diagnosed with CTE has become impossible to ignore. Even the NFL finally backed down after years of denying there was any connection.

So, maybe instead of relying on the morally lazy argument that football players make the choice to play, we should try to figure out why we want to watch this train wreck of concussions, corruption, and macho bullshit.

Does football have to be this way? I don't know. I hope not. Safer tackling techniques, greater awareness of CTE, and less "suck it up" ignorance would all help. The Seattle Seahawks have apparently overhauled the entire culture of a typical NFL team. They practice meditation and yoga. There is a staff psychotherapist who encourages players to talk about their anxieties and frustrations. Instead of humiliating players who drop a pass or miss a blocking assignment, the coaching staff works through the problem in a rational way, trying to improve a player's performance. All this seems like a step in the right direction. Not only is it sensible, it's also effective—the Seahawks are now at the top of their division.

Seattle is a long way from Oklahoma, where I hear from mutual acquaintances that Mike has established himself as a very successful businessman. I bet he's probably forgotten about Josh and the tablespoon. But I haven't—and we can thank Richie Incognito for that.

HORSES AND DAGGER

Behind the closed-door passage of the laws that made horse
slaughter legal in Oklahoma

By *Jennie Lloyd*

OFF RURAL HIGHWAY 16, along a dusty stretch of Bristow sits
one of the largest live auction houses in Oklahoma. At the mouth of
a wide gravel driveway, weathered plastic figures of a horse and steer
greet passers-by with a stoic gaze. Black metal letters stand out against
rust-colored rock: Mid America Stockyards.

For 40 years, Mid America has drawn packed houses to their
Saturday cattle sale and horse auctions every other Monday. On busy
auction days, three sets of stadium bleacher seats become a loud, moving sea of cowboy hats, well-worn plaid, and overalls. The earthy tang
of horseshit and dirty boots steams up the stale, warm air. State flags
flank both sides of the auctioneer who speaks and calls in an old-hand
showboating twang.

Experienced riding horses, skittish unbroken colts, and head-down
workhorses—plus mules, donkeys, and even llamas—emerge from a
whitewashed gate one at a time. They twitch their tails and ears under
the lights, as the gathered crowd of grimacing men and gray-haired
matrons bid on the animals.

Among these bidders are experienced "kill buyers." These are the
people who frequent auction houses to buy cheap horses by the pound,

as cheap as a nickel a pound at Mid America, then sell them to slaughterhouses for a profit.

Jerry and Helen Marie Varner have managed their highly profitable and well-respected family auction and cattle business for decades. The Varners see more than a thousand head of cattle come through their barns each week.

House Representative Skye McNiel, R-Bristow, still helps out with her grandparents' business on Fridays. With her pretty blonde hair, blue eyes, and big smile, she serves hearty breakfasts and lunches at the stockyards' café. Earlier this year, McNiel became a polarizing political figure when she introduced House Bill 1999, the bill that has opened Oklahoma to horse slaughter.

TOO QUICK, TOO QUIET

On February 20, 2013, HB 1999 passed in the House easily, 82-14, and officially ended a 50-year state ban on horse slaughter.

While McNiel's bill sped through the House, a similar bill introduced by State Senator Mark Allen, R-Spiro, passed in the Oklahoma Senate with equal ease (SB 375 was approved 38-6).

McNiel garnered wide support for her bill among the deep-pocketed agricultural interests in the state, as well as the Oklahoma Farm Bureau and the American Quarter Horse Association. Calls and emails to Oklahoma Quarter Horse Association were not returned. According to national export data, quarter horses make up about 70 percent of all horses sent slaughter.

The bills passed quickly and with relatively little debate; a little too quickly and quietly for Representative Jeannie McDaniel, D-Tulsa.

"It just sort of snuck in quickly, and bang it was gone," McDaniel said.

The aftermath of the bills' initial passage caused an intense rift between opponents of horse slaughter and those who support the legislation. McDaniel said her email inbox is overflowing. The majority of McDaniel's—all urban—constituents who have contacted her regarding HB 1999 are "overwhelmingly opposed," she said.

McNiel said she's received a lot of hateful and negative feedback, including a death threat currently under investigation by the OSBI.

"People will say things on a computer that they won't say to your face," McNiel said. "The Capitol police watch me when I'm in the Capitol Rotunda," and anywhere on the grounds. She said she fears threats made against her family and daughters. But that doesn't mean she'll back down.

Governor Mary Fallin signed HB 1999 into law late Friday afternoon, March 29, 2013.

Fallin said HB 1999 would "allow the humane, regulated processing of horses."

The law will go into effect November 1, 2013.

PUBLIC OPPOSED

Oddly, legislators' support for horse slaughter far outweighs that of public opinion, according to a mid-March SoonerPoll commissioned by the Humane Society of the United States (HSUS) and the American Society for the Prevention of Cruelty to Animals (ASPCA). A strong 66 percent of Oklahoma voters opposed the passage of proposed legislation allowing for the slaughter of horses in the state. Most of those opposed—88 percent—are strongly opposed, the poll concluded. More interesting was that respondents in rural areas opposed horse slaughter legislation at high rates, not unlike their urban counterparts. In rural counties, 65.1 percent of those surveyed opposed the bills, with 69.6 percent of respondents in the Tulsa metropolitan area opposed and 64.3 percent opposed in the Oklahoma City metropolitan area.

The bills achieve a rare feat today—people of all political stripes hate on Oklahoma's horse slaughter bills at high rates. Independent respondents were opposed or strongly opposed at the highest rate, 72.5 percent, Democrats at 67.6 percent and Republicans, 63.4 percent. Conservatives and moderates? They both oppose horse slaughter.

Horse-loving Americans gave a collective pearl-clutch when a YouTube video went viral in March. In the video, Valley Meat Company employee Tim Sappington is shown in cowboy hat and boots, cursing animal rights activists before shooting a black and brown colt between the eyes with a .48. The New Mexico man watches the horse drop to its side, then he walks toward the camera and says, "Good."

The video outraged animal lovers coast to coast, garnering headlines and sparking fierce opposition to horse slaughter. Despite public opposition, Sappington's employer, Valley Meat Company, may be permitted to slaughter horses within the next few weeks.

Though HB 1999 is now state law, a ban on selling horsemeat for human consumption would remain in effect statewide. In Oklahoma, we can kill horses. We just can't eat them.

HORSES SELL BY THE POUND

After the live auction is over, kill buyers—also known as contract buyers—turn a profit by selling the newly acquired horses to slaughter facilities across the border in Canada or Mexico. There, the meat is processed for sale overseas. Some horsemeat is sold back to U.S. zoos as lion and tiger feed, though its use in pet food was banned in the 1970s.

Nine million horses live in the U.S., and Oklahoma is home to about 326,000, according to the Oklahoma Farm Bureau. Oklahoma City is considered the horse-show capital of the world, while Purcell, Oklahoma, boasts itself the Quarter Horse capital of the world. More than 12,000 Oklahomans work with, for, or around horses. Equines are our workmates and companions, not our entrées or appetizers.

However, some countries consider horseflesh a delicacy, priced on par with veal. The meat is much leaner than beef, contains no cholesterol and is rich in iron. In China, people eat horsemeat by the ton (about half a million tons a year). Italian gourmands crave tender, thin slices of *prosciutto di cavallo*. A Puglia, Italy, recipe for "horse chops," or *baciole alla barese*, calls for rolled and seasoned pieces of horsemeat to pan sear in a coat of lard, red wine, and tomato sauce. In France, a hearty stew, or *pot-au-feu de cheval*, must simmer all afternoon to marry together the flavors of fresh garden vegetables and a horse's collar meat. The flesh is also frequently smoked and made into cold cuts or squished into burger patties.

Currently, no horse slaughterhouses operate in the U.S., and the last three facilities shuttered in 2007. Since then, the number of horses imported by Canada and Mexico increased astronomically, 148 percent and 660 percent respectively, according to a June 2011 report released by the Government Accountability Office (GAO). In 2010, nearly 138,000 horses were sent to Canada and Mexico for slaughter, about the same number that were sent to slaughter before the ban was put into place, the report found.

The GAO analysis of horse-sale data estimated that closing U.S. horse slaughterhouses caused horse prices to drop on lower- and medium-end horses to the tune of 8–10 percent. Higher-priced horses held their market value, while the economic downturn repressed the prices of all horses by 4–5 percent, the report estimated.

Profits on horsemeat within the food industry are hard to analyze. Food margins are thin to start, and companies are always looking for a cheaper way to process meats. "Supply chains have become vast and unwieldy," in a system where meat "now travels across multiple borders and through myriad companies," according to an editorial in *Financial Times*.

IN THE KILL BOX

Pro-slaughter and horse advocates agree on one thing: the way other countries operate horse slaughterhouses can be, and often are, sub-par, suspect, and—as a quick search on YouTube will reveal—revolting.

Cattle and livestock expert Temple Grandin, the autistic "cattle whisperer," has asserted in a statement that she believes Mexican slaughterhouses, where thousands of horses are shipped from live auctions like Mid America each year, are inhumane.

"The worst outcome from an animal welfare perspective is a horse going to a local Mexican abattoir," Grandin wrote in a statement on her website, grandin.com. "Once a horse crosses the Mexican border, there is no way to monitor how it's transported or slaughtered. A plant in the U.S. would be monitored by the USDA/FSIS, and the conditions for both transport and slaughter would be better."

Though Grandin does support ethical, well-run, and humane slaughterhouses in the U.S., she condemns south-of-the-border slaughterhouses because they use a small knife, known as a puntilla. These knives are used to sever the spinal cord, so horses are paralyzed and unable to breathe. The animals are then hoisted upside down, awake and able to feel pain, until they bleed out.

Canadian abattoirs have been repeatedly accused of ethical violations as well. Though they eschew the puntilla in favor of a quicker death,

Canadian kill boxes can still lead to a terrifying death for easily panicked horses. More intelligent than cows and with twice the blood, horses simply aren't the same as cattle. When a frightened horse is dragged from a pen into a kill box, he will often thrash his head against the sides of the wide stall in an attempt to escape. This thrashing motion makes it difficult to aim the captive-bolt gun at the horse's head.

It is not a simple, easy, or quick singular blow to the head for many horses. Abattoir employees may shoot a frantic horse three or four times before he dies. Even then, undercover investigations by animal welfare organizations show signs of life in some horses as they are strung up, even after being shot multiple times.

In 2011, the Canadian Horse Defence Coalition (CHDC) released undercover footage and videos of a Quebec slaughterhouse. The footage showed everything from the misidentification and often missing information on the horses, to gross failures during assembly-line captive-bolt gun use. At the slaughterhouse they investigated, at least 40 percent of the horses in the stun box were not rendered immediately unconscious, according to CHDC findings.

In 2009, Humane Society International (HSI) reported 93,000 horses were slaughtered in Canada. The organization also expressed concern about the treatment of horses while they are transported from live auction to slaughterhouse. On these long trips, horses are loaded unceremoniously onto trailers, where Canadian regulations allow them to ride for up to 36 hours without food or water, according to HSI.

TOUGH TIMES, TOUGHER MEASURES

"In Oklahoma—as in other states—abuse is tragically common among horses that are reaching the end of their natural lives," Fallin said after she signed HB 1999. "Many horses are abandoned or left to starve to death."

Pro-slaughter advocates frequently say it's the only option for strapped horse owners. Times are tough, and horses cost thousands per year in care and upkeep. U.S. slaughterhouses are sold as the perfect solution to the problem of abandoned, neglected, and aging horses. Unraveling this claim is difficult because there are no firm statistics or tracking in place to accurately count abandoned horses.

The governor referenced the 68-page GAO report to support her stance. "Comprehensive, national data are lacking," the report stated, "But state, local government, and animal welfare organizations report a rise in investigations for horse neglect and more abandoned horses since 2007."

The cases of horse neglect the GAO referenced were attained through interviews and anecdotal evidence. Pet-Abuse.com tracks cases of animal cruelty and abandonment in each state, though most are unconfirmed allegations. In Oklahoma, nine people reported the malnourishment, neglect or theft of at least 40 horses between 2011 and 2012. No reports have been filed in 2013.

For-profit slaughterhouses are a far cry from humane euthanasia, said Oklahoma City horse advocate Stephanie Graham. The cost of a quick, painless euthanasia, an injection given by a veterinarian, and disposal of the remains cost approximately $225, according to HSUS.

Graham grew up just outside Yukon, on a wheat farm where her family kept American Quarter Horses and Appaloosas.

"I grew up riding, showing, training, the whole works," she said. "I always had my hand in the dirt or on a horse."

Graham, a chronic pain specialist, has found herself immersed in battling recent Oklahoma legislation that would pave the way for horse slaughter facilities to open in the state.

"I wouldn't call myself an advocate," she said. "I'd call myself a decent human being. There's nothing radical about that."

People like Graham enumerate legitimate concerns, especially regarding the treatment of horses that are sent to slaughter across the border. It's a concern shared by McNiel, who also condemns the "horrible" treatment horses often receive during transport to slaughter. She said a slaughterhouse in the U.S. would save horses the long distances they travel in cramped trailers.

On March 26, People for the Ethical Treatment of Animals called out Oklahoma agricultural officials after an undercover investigator found serious violations during a ride with a kill buyer through Oklahoma. The kill buyer admitted he falsified health forms for the horses in his trailer, according to a PETA statement. The horses were transported from Iowa, though Kansas and Missouri, and then into Oklahoma before they headed to Texas. The kill buyer said a veterinarian taught him how to falsely "certify" the horses in his trailer were free of equine infectious anemia (EIA), a potentially fatal viral disease with no known cure or vaccine. The potentially infected horses were unloaded onto a crowded feedlot in Stroud, Oklahoma, PETA stated.

Agriculture Secretary Jim Reese said he and other officials are "aware" of the allegations, and that they are being investigated by the state's multi-county grand jury, according to the *Oklahoman*. Reese told the newspaper that the jury is also looking into allegations of stolen property, concealing stolen property, and transporting stolen property across state lines, among other crimes.

CAN'T TALK FACTS TO EMOTION

The daughter of prominent Bristow cattle ranchers, Representative McNiel said she loved saddling up horses on Sunday afternoons. "We are predominantly cattle people," she said, "But we love being on horseback."

Her husband, Pecos McNiel, trains horses and is a talented auctioneer, and the couple's two daughters have horses, too. "We understand how you can love a horse," she said. "We get that. We love our cattle, show pigs, show lambs."

But where horse advocates make a strong distinction between cow and horse, McNiel said, "It's OK for cattle to be processed, and it's an identical method for a horse."

She said she finds it difficult to maintain common ground with opponents of HB 1999. "Our opponents are based on emotion," McNiel said, "We can't talk facts to them."

To McNiel and other pro-slaughter advocates, capitalism is the answer. A demand for quality horsemeat in foreign markets plus an excess of unwanted healthy horses in the U.S. equals potential profits. And those profits grow once you subtract the expensive transport of the horses out of the country. It's simple. Her opponents, she said, "want to make it very absurd and very gruesome."

About 21,000 horses from Oklahoma are shipped to slaughter facilities across the border, with 160,000 ultimately sent to slaughter nationwide last year, McNiel said.

Even if legislation is passed and the ban on horse slaughter is lifted in Oklahoma, McNiel said she doesn't know of any companies who are interested in opening a facility in the state.

She agreed we have a "problem" with transport and other ethical violations in foreign abattoirs, "and we need to address it," she said. "We may need to look at population control, look at people who abandon or abuse horses. But we can't do it through fear. We need to do it through facts."

LIFTING MORAN'S AMENDMENT

Representative McNiel explained the language for HB 1999 has been simmering since 2006, she said, "when the U.S. federal government pulled funding for USDA inspections."

McNiel is referencing the federal government's effective prohibition on horse slaughter nationwide since 2006. A small piece of legislation attached to an annual agricultural spending bill effectively blocked funding for USDA inspections of horse slaughter. No inspection, no business, no deal.

The Moran Amendment would reinstate a 2006 ban on the slaughter and consumption. It is named after U.S. House Representative Jim Moran, a Virginia Democrat and co-chair of Congressional Animal Protection Caucus.

In 2011, the annual spending bill included language that would have continued the federal ban on funding for horse slaughterhouse inspections. However, before the bill reached President Barack Obama's desk, it was stripped of the ban that was so easily approved in 2006. The president signed the bill into law on November 17, 2011. And just like that, a five-year ban on horsemeat inspections was lifted.

Valley Meat Company, the slaughterhouse that employs Sappington in New Mexico, could be ready to slaughter horses in a matter of weeks. Since then, a number of cities in other states have applied for horse slaughter inspection permits, including: Larkspur, Colorado; Gallatin, Missouri; Woodbury, Tennessee; and Sigourney, Iowa, according to *Food Safety News.*

As a response to Valley Meat Company's application to slaughter horses in New Mexico, Representative Moran called on Department of Agriculture Secretary Tom Vilsack to deny permit applications for horse slaughter facilities. In the March 25 open letter to Vilsack, Moran wrote, "Horses are not raised as food animals and are routinely given substances that are banned by the FDA from administration to animals destined for human consumption.

"At a time when USDA's budget is diminished by budget cuts and sequestration ... every dollar spent at horse slaughter plants would divert necessary resources away from beef, chicken, and pork inspections—meat actually consumed by Americans."

Moran urged Vilsack to "exercise all available options to prevent the resumption of this industry."

Moran has also promised to fight for a federal ban on horse slaughter and for the reinstatement of his amendment. "I will be working with my colleagues in the coming weeks to include that language in the final Fiscal Year 2014 appropriations bill," he promised in a March 8 statement. One meat processing plant, Oklahoma Meat Company, in Washington, Oklahoma, (just a few miles south of Norman in rural McClain County) has applied for an extension of USDA inspections. The facility already processes cows, sheep and goats, according to the company's USDA application filed on May 24, 2012. The Oklahoma slaughterhouse differs from other applications in that it is owned by locals. Almost all horse slaughter facilities in the U.S. have been owned by Belgian, French, or Dutch interests.

Another measure is also circulating in federal houses of congress, called the Safeguard American Food Exports (SAFE) Act, which would shut down any possibility of an American slaughterhouse and slam closed the borders on kill buyers shipping horses to Canada or Mexico. The bipartisan legislation was written in response to the scandal in Europe, when horse meat was discovered in fast food meals after it was mislabeled as beef.

WHEN PICKENS MET BACON

Back in 2006, a more definitive ban on horse slaughter was also being promoted as a permanent solution.

One looming Oklahoma figure, T. Boone Pickens, the billionaire oilman and Oklahoma State University alumni, championed the Ameri-

HORSES AND DAGGER

can Horse Slaughter Prevention Act, and became an outspoken opponent of horse slaughter at home and abroad. Despite disappointing his former colleagues in the cattle industry, Pickens told *Time* magazine in July 2006, "I don't like it. And I'm going to do everything I can to stop it."

One of the people he met during his quest to end horse slaughter in the U.S., was the outspoken former mayor of a small Texas town. Pickens was moved by Bacon's story, and talked about her frequently.

Bacon ran for mayor after watching her beloved small Texas town fight for years to rid themselves of a horse slaughterhouse called Dallas Crown. Bacon spearheaded efforts to shut down the plant, which closed down in 2007. Though she is no longer mayor, Bacon still speaks out about the horror story of Dallas Crown.

"I'm fifth generation Kaufman," she said proudly, in one of a few rapid-fire recent phone conversations. "I had an exuberant, empowering childhood."

But, Bacon said, "The horse slaughter plant was a black eye" on her town. So she ran for mayor, in part to fight Dallas Crown. And she won on both counts.

When she got into office, she said, "We were about to have to build a new wastewater treatment plant", plus update their sewer system to the tune of $2 million, "if we were lucky."

Horses are frequently treated with antibiotics and worming medications toxic to humans, and because equines have twice the volume of blood as a cow (with less meat), wastewater and sewage problems were frequent and egregious. Hundreds of gallons of blood overwhelmed the small Texas town's municipal capabilities. The blood and carcasses never seemed to stay put.

BLOOD BUBBLING UP IN BATHTUBS

Kaufman residents who lived near Dallas Crown frequently reported blood spills in the roadway and in ditches, as well as blood bubbling up in bathtubs and toilets. Residents' photos reveal horse carcasses and bones on the plant's property. Bacon said the stench of death was horrendous. The blood and the carcasses attracted hundreds of vultures, cockroaches, and other scavengers to the area.

JENNIE LLOYD

Kaufman couldn't shake its reputation as "the place where they kill horses." Bacon said business investors would visit, but never call back. "The standard answer was, 'It's just not a good fit,'" she said.

Dallas Crown employed about 42 people, who were paid $7-$10 per hour for the undesirable dirty work that went on inside. The city gained nothing in sales tax revenue, while the plant's property taxes were only $1600-$1700 per year; it wasn't nearly enough to cover the city's costs to support the plant municipally.

The local hospital installed special water filters because the water still wasn't acceptable after treatment. Additionally, hospital administrators were "extremely unhappy because the prevailing winds carried a terrible odor there," Bacon said. But the smell was inescapable almost everywhere in Kaufman.

A hundred percent of the people who lived in the vicinity of Dallas Crown signed a petition condemning the plant as a nuisance alongside the city's city council, Bacon said.

When the plant shuttered, Chevideco left $916,000 in unpaid fines after 19 months of continual violations.

"Horse slaughter, it's a burden on taxpayers," Bacon said. "It's not good jobs, and it's going to hurt a community, not help."

She believes that a horse slaughter plant in Oklahoma "absolutely" would have the same problems. Even after the plant closed, the city had to deal with watershed cleanup issues related to the horse blood, urine, and waste.

Once a foreign-owned plant sets up shop in a rural area, shutting them down again can be extremely difficult. "We were hamstrung by their deep pockets," Bacon said. "I don't think anybody realizes. God, it's just almost impossible.

"We had so much evidence," she continued. "But it was not sufficient help to get us out of this."

An obscure state law banning horse slaughter in the state of Texas allowed Kaufman to finally rid itself of the plant. Dallas Crown is owned by an international conglomerate headquartered in Belgium. This allowed the slaughterhouse to dodge federal taxes, and made confrontation difficult.

Chevideco appealed their case all the way to the Texas Supreme Court. "It's only because the Supreme Court refused to hear their case that we got rid of them."

McNiel said she believes Dallas Crown was an anomaly. "Can you tell me any industry where every single person acted perfect?" she asked. "One bad business out of all these hundreds shouldn't give us a black eye for all eternity."

After Governor Fallin signed McNiel's bill, she stated, "Should there ever be a processing facility planned, my administration will work with the Department of Agriculture to ensure it is run appropriately, follows all state and local laws, and is not a burden or hazard to the community."

The governor also noted that communities could block the construction and operation of horse slaughter plants "at the local level."

BACK AT THE BARN

Back at the barn on auction day, bidders at Mid America Stockyards hold up small square cards, and conduct the comfortable call and response between auctioneer and buyer. According to HSI figures, more than 50 percent of horses sold at rural auctions like North America end up in a slaughterhouse.

After the deals are done and the bleachers have emptied, horses are loaded onto trailers in the lavender dusk of Oklahoma back roads; some head on to home pastures, others turn-signal onto highways that lead to places unknown.

SNAKES ON A PLAIN

Undercover at Oklahoma's rattlesnake roundups, where the capture, killing, and consumption of deadly reptiles are all fun and games

By *Holly Wall*

I STOOD SHAKING in the center of a wooden 9-by-12-foot pit, surrounded on all sides by about 250 western diamondback rattlesnakes.

"Just be still, and stay calm," a man in a black cowboy hat reassured me.

Teddy Richey and his son T.J., from Thackerville, Oklahoma, are members of the Outlaw Handlers. They travel to small-town rattlesnake roundups in Oklahoma and Texas with their stunt show, at once educating and astounding festivalgoers with feats of bravery that involve live, sometimes agitated (sometimes nearly dead), rattlesnakes. Their ringleader is Mike Darrow. He wears a black cowboy hat, too, but he's shorter and trimmer than Teddy, his tan face accessorized by wide, wire-framed glasses and a neat gray mustache.

Mike's the one who got me into this mess, and he's the one who was sliding coiled rattlesnakes toward me and arranging them at my feet. He carefully rested their rattles against the toes of my too-thin leather boots.

"I won't let them strike," Mike promised me, reading the fear on my face. Another handler, the only woman on the team, took photos with my phone.

I stood as still as I could, doing my best to breathe and act relaxed. At the same time I was scared that my breath would cause a shift in my hips or ankles, a welcoming gesture for a snake just waiting to sink its fangs.

Once the snakes settled around my feet—six of them circled me—T.J. wrapped what he promised was a non-poisonous snake around my shoulders. Either end rested in the crooks between my thumbs and forefingers, and I held it gently as it stared into my eyes, flicking its forked tongue.

I glanced down at the snakes coiled around my feet. Their rattles hummed against my shoes. Then something, ever so lightly, brushed against the back of my knee. I didn't move—stopped breathing, even. My heart pounded.

"I'm done," I said. "Get me out of here."

Small towns in Oklahoma build their yearly festivals upon whatever gimmick happens to be native, in one way or another, to the area. In Porter, it's peaches; in Stilwell, it's strawberries; in Prague, it's the Bohemian treat kolaches; and in southwestern Oklahoma, where the dry, desert ecosystem seems worlds away, despite being a two-and-a-half-hour drive from Green Country, it's rattlesnakes.

Oklahoma is home to seven species of venomous snakes, five of which are rattlesnakes. The western diamondback and prairie rattlesnakes are most common, and they're the ones, especially the former, that hunters are after. Western massasauga, pigmy, and timber (known locally as velvet-tail) rattlesnakes are also native to Oklahoma, though they're becoming increasingly rare. Cottonmouth and copperhead snakes are the other venomous species native to the state, more common in the east.

The western diamondback and prairie rattlesnakes prefer the dry, rocky grasslands of western Oklahoma. They make their homes in the gypsum bluffs, slithering behind and underneath rock that juts from the hills to make their dens, which they share with up to 100 other snakes. Around October, when nighttime temperatures begin to drop below 50 degrees, they retreat to their dens, where they stay until they can feel the rocks above them begin to warm under the sun's rays, usually in March. But they're known to take advantage of a warm winter day, to slither out onto a rock to sun themselves. That's when they fall prey to birds, coyotes, and mountain lions—and to hunters.

SNAKES ON A PLAIN

Farmers and ranchers in Okeene—in Blaine County, about 90 minutes west and north of Oklahoma City—hunted snakes decades before someone got the bright idea to build a festival around the practice. Men used shotguns and women garden hoes, and together, they'd scour their land for snakes, ridding it, their cattle, and their children of the threat of the creatures' deadly venom. If they killed a really big one, they might hang it up on the side of their wagon or truck and drive into town to show it off.

In the 1930s, Orville van Goelker, publicity manager for the Okeene Milling Company, saw a group gathered around a pickup truck in town one day. In the bed was a large, dead rattlesnake. Van Goelker thought he could draw an even bigger crowd with a live snake or two. So he, along with the rest of the Junior Chamber of Commerce, of which he just happened to be the president, organized the town's first rattlesnake roundup in 1939.

They kept it small, Anthony Felder told me, because they weren't sure what kind of trouble they might be getting into. Anthony is 84 and the unofficial Okeene Rattlesnake Roundup historian. He zipped over to me on a borrowed motorized scooter on the first Sunday in May, the last day of this year's festival. He saw me browsing old photographs of roundups past and offered to tell me the stories that went along with the pictures. He remembers the first rattlesnake festival—his dad was one of the snake-hunting locals. A few years later, when Anthony turned 14, he was, too.

The Jaycees shot for an attendance of 250 for their second festival. When they topped that number—and no one was fanged—they added attractions to draw larger crowds. Within five years, they were making a profit and pumping money back into the town via community service projects. Throughout the 1950s and '60s, they attracted crowds upwards of 25,000.

Okeene claims—and so far, no one's refuted it—to be the oldest rattlesnake roundup in the country. Today, there are six festivals in Oklahoma, and several more in Texas, Alabama, Georgia, Kansas, Pennsylvania, and New Mexico. Okeene's Jaycees helped several other Oklahoma towns get their festivals up and running.

In Okeene I perused the vendors' booths, the carnival games, and the rides. I bought a raffle ticket from the Blue Star Mothers and scarfed

HOLLY WALL

a loaded cheeseburger before I made my way toward a blue metal barn, where I was told I'd find the snakes. I gave a guy about my age five dollars and let him clumsily wrap a hot-pink paper bracelet around my right wrist. Hand-painted signs warned me of the danger ahead, inside the Den of Death.

The moment my foot hit the barn's dusty threshold and my nostrils filled with snake stench, the symphony of a hundred buzzing rattles was interrupted by a long, shrill scream.

A gaggle of teenage girls crowded around a bloodied butcher station, where teenage and 20-something locals were processing snake meat. It would be bagged and sold, raw or battered and deep-fried, to hungry and adventurous festivalgoers in five-dollar baskets.

The station began at a blood-splattered tree stump. The young guys doing the bulk of the dirty work were letting some giggling girls, with their heavy eye shadow and short shorts, chop off the heads. A kid in a blue T-shirt and ball cap pinned the snake to the stump and waited for one of the girls, still standing a safe three feet away from the thing, to swing an ax at a spot just behind its head. Every girl, every time, would swing, scream, drop the ax, and run.

Each swing lacked the conviction required to take a life, so the snake's head dangled, hanging on by a thread of skin and meat. Its body writhed while the boy tried to talk the girl into finishing the job. She couldn't, or wouldn't, so he'd strike the final blow, letting the head hit the floor while he passed the body, still squirming, to another boy standing over a metal trashcan, which was bloodstained enough to be used as a horror movie prop. Painted on the side were a couple of snakes and the words "BUTCHER SHOP."

The boy slid a pair of utility scissors into the cavity where the head once was, slicing the skin along the snake's belly in a straight line as blood fell into the trashcan. Reaching inside the snake, he pulled out a long sac containing the snake's entrails and tossed it on a table nearby, where a handful of eggs, a gall bladder, and a still-beating heart attracted plenty of attention from other attendees. Another kid affixed one of the severed heads onto the side of a Styrofoam cup, holding it high for folks taking photos

Once the guts were out, the guy pulled the snake's skin away from the white, almost translucent, meat beneath. Working slowly at first, then building speed and momentum, he tore off the entire skin at once, leaving it intact and still attached to the rattle. He cut the snake from the last bit of skin and hung the skin to dry, next to about a dozen others, on a string of clothesline. Later it would be rolled up and sold.

The meat passed to a more pristine area of the butcher shop, where it smelled of bleach and there wasn't a drop of blood in sight. There, a plastic-gloved girl was portioning the snake, chopping it with a cleaver into several three- or four-inch pieces.

I first tasted snake meat a couple of weeks earlier, at the Waynoka Rattlesnake Hunt. My boyfriend, my kids, and I were first in line when the call rang out that meat was ready. We paid $10 for two portions of rattlesnake—one battered and chicken fried, the other smoked.

The first big bite of fried rattlesnake was a mouthful of bones. I searched with my tongue for any smidgen of meat. When I found it, after spitting several tiny bones back into the Styrofoam bowl, it was tough and nearly impossible to chew. The meat itself didn't have much flavor—it certainly didn't taste like chicken, which was what we'd been promised. The closest thing I could compare it to was alligator meat (no offense to alligators).

The smoked snake was tender and easier to eat, but it had the imitation flavor of Liquid Smoke. The third bite tasted rancid, like the stuff my mom put on my fingernails when I was a kid to get me to stop sucking my thumb. After that, I didn't eat any more, but the fellas with me polished off what was left. My sons liked it enough that they probably would have eaten more, and they were certainly hungry enough, but I suggested we get a corndog at the carnival instead.

The butcher shop in Okeene is the kind of thing that has folks like Ned Bruha and members of Rise Against Rattlesnake Roundups pressing local law enforcement to put an end to what they call felony animal abuse. Their objections are many: Rattlesnake season is March 1 through June 30, but many hunters admit to venturing out on a warm winter day, catching more snakes than they would in the spring. A snake caught in mid-December will likely spend the months leading up to April and May's festivals in a bucket, box, or burlap bag—without food or water.

Once the snakes make it to the festival, they're hungry, fatigued, and dehydrated. If they're taken to the festivals in Apache or Mangum—or, until this year, Waurika—they might be one of the few chosen to entertain guests of the festival's photo booth. With that honor comes the painful process of fang removal and mouth sewing, a guarantee of safety to the folks willing to fork over five dollars for a souvenir photo.

Bruha and others have beseeched local law enforcement, county and state officials, representatives of the Oklahoma Department of Wildlife, the state attorney general, and the governor in hopes that someone will intervene and end the practice. So far, they've been unsuccessful. Bruha even sent a letter to President Obama, only to receive a generic form reply.

The festivals generate $5,000 to $35,000 annually for the organizations that host them—either the Jaycees, who use part of the profits to purchase schools supplies and Christmas gifts for needy children, or the local volunteer fire department, which wouldn't have equipment or supplies without its local festival. Ten times as much money gets pumped into the local economy by visitors who also eat, sleep, and pump gas within city limits. Because of that, and because, in Bible-reading, cattle-ranching Oklahoma, snakes are considered the devil incarnate, no one minds too much when a few of them get their mouths sewn shut—or a few hundred find their way to slaughterhouses.

"Although a rattlesnake is not as cute and cuddly as a dog, Oklahoma animal cruelty statutes do not differentiate," Bruha wrote in a letter to Attorney General Scott Pruitt when he filed a citizen's complaint with the multicounty grand jury division. "Using pliers to remove the fangs, sewing a rattlesnake's mouth shut, and depriving them of food and water is a felony in Oklahoma. You and the rest of Oklahoma lawmakers and law enforcement have ignored thousands of requests from around the world asking you to enforce existing Oklahoma laws."

Oklahoma categorizes rattlesnakes as animals—not pests or rodents, like Texas does—so the state's animal cruelty laws apply. Those laws say: "Any person who shall willfully or maliciously overdrive, overload, torture, destroy or kill, or cruelly beat or injure, maim or mutilate, any animal in subjugation or captivity... shall be guilty of a felony and shall be punished by imprisonment in the State Penitentiary not exceeding five (5) years, or by imprisonment in the county jail not exceeding one (1) year, or by a fine not exceeding Five Hundred Dollars ($500.00)."

Bruha hasn't had any luck getting anyone to enforce the law when it comes to rattlesnakes. Patrick Abitbol said no one cares about rattlesnakes enough to care whether they're protected from cruelty. Abitbol is a retired assistant district attorney whose relentless pursuit of justice for abused women, children, and animals earned him the nickname "Pit Bull." He has volunteered to advise Bruha and others in their pursuit of justice.

"My feeling is that it will end; we're just not at the public opinion stage of accomplishing anything," Abitbol said. "I don't believe anything will resolve itself until the public itself has an outcry that this is not acceptable behavior. There's no reason for it. You would no more allow a dog to have its mouth sewn shut, even if you were going to euthanize it tomorrow. There's no purpose."

Joe Dorman, a state representative and the recipient of many of Bruha's pleas, has, off and on for years, worked in the snake pit at the Apache Rattlesnake Roundup. He lauds the event as an educational and economic opportunity. Only a couple of the snakes' mouths are sewn shut, and in the end, they're slaughtered, and their meat, skin, and entrails are sold. "Every part of the snake used," he said. "The organs are ground and used for spices in Asian culture. It's no different than any other animal production.

"I think there's some misunderstanding with what happens at hunts," he continued. "It's about getting out and understanding the culture. But there have been some concerns, and we're taking steps to address those issues. Hopefully, there can be an agreement reached so there is no animal cruelty issue at these festivals."

In 1988, the Oklahoma Department of Wildlife Conservation, which has since refused or ignored Bruha's requests to take action against the festivals, issued a report on the rattlesnake roundups, calling "crowding and water deprivation of snakes captured several weeks prior to the events"—which results in suffocation for many—and the defanging and mouth-sewing, plus the treatment of the snakes at the butcher shops, cruel. "Sewing is no doubt done with the animal fully conscious and undoubtedly is a painful, traumatic process for the snake," the report stated. Bruha claims some festival officials have admitted to placing the snakes in a freezer for 15 or so minutes before sewing their mouths shut, to slow them down a bit.

Bruha said many of the law enforcement and elected officials he petitioned admitted to him that some of what is happening at the roundups is cruel and, yes, illegal. But they don't put an end to it because it's too profitable for the small towns they represent, and they say that if they interfere, they'll be out of a job.

In Claxton, Georgia, organizers of the Claxton Rattlesnake Round-up have stopped catching and killing wild snakes. They've reinvented their event as a wildlife festival and use captive snakes from local zoos to provide an educational event. John Jensen, senior wildlife biologist for the Georgia Department of Natural Resources, told the *Savannah Morning News* that the decision came after "years and years of pressure" from several local groups. "For eastern diamondbacks, the biggest threat is habitat loss," he told the paper. "But then you tack on that they're killed by anybody who sees them and harvested for roundups and harvested for skins. Another main thing is these events contribute to passing along to younger people the idea that wildlife should be treated this way. People should recognize they're potentially dangerous, but they're part of the ecosystem."

Bruha and others would like to see the roundups in Oklahoma make a similar change, and they say the events would still be as profitable for the local economies—if not the snake sellers—if they made the roundups no-kill.

"I do not consider myself an animal rights activist whatsoever, but the animals still deserve better," Bruha said.

In Waurika, where I was charmed into the snake pit, the roundup is organized by and benefits the volunteer fire department. This year was the first in 52 that they didn't sew snakes' mouths shut. The activists got to them, Stephen Dyer told me. They were tired of being bothered, said the town's only paid firefighter, and they decided it wasn't worth it.

In Waurika, rattlesnake roundups have paid for two new pumper trucks for the fire department, as well as a new tanker and a new grass rig. "We're as big as Duncan," Rickey Porterfield boasted from the driver's seat of his white pickup. Earlier, the volunteer firefighter and snake hunter took me to a spot of private land, 700 acres' worth, about four miles outside of town, where a group of festivalgoers hunted for rattlers. We stopped

Snakes on a Plain

by the town's fire department to see its shiny new trucks. Rickey, a big guy with a wild mane of curly white-gray hair, is one of 17 volunteer firefighters in Waurika. He's been on the job for 21 years; he'll retire in two. When he does, he'll likely retire from rattlesnake hunting as well.

Rickey had his first experience with fire in the 1970s, before he joined the department. There was a three-building fire on Main Street, and one of the firefighters grabbed him and told him to hold the water cannon. He figures he sat on it for eight or nine hours. He wasn't scared then, he said, and fire doesn't scare him now. "Fire's a lot like rattlesnakes," he told me on the way back to the festival's main drag. "You've gotta respect 'em."

PETRO STATE

How oil became king in Oklahoma

BY *James McGirk*

BETWEEN 1910 AND 1960, as the population of the city of Tulsa swelled from 18,000 to 261,000, the world was being transformed. Mind-bending inventions were coming online: Airplanes were buzzing the skies, cars and trucks were zipping across the country, phone lines were installed, movie theaters were sprouting up, diseases were cured, atoms were split, and spaceships were launched. The world was becoming forever more mechanized and strange. Artists and architects and designers wanted to incorporate all of this into their work. Almost all of this fantastic stuff was coming courtesy of a compact fuel source drawn from deep within the earth: petroleum.

Tulsa's strange buildings are totems to the oceans of hydrocarbon bubbling beneath the prairies. And not just Tulsa. Throughout Oklahoma's 107 years of statehood (and about 50 years prior to becoming a state), a large swath of the population has devoted itself to turning the state inside out, bringing oil and gas to the surface, refining it, and sending it out all over the world. The logistics involved, and the flows and counter-flows of capital and labor, have radically reshaped the landscape and infrastructure of the state. No other state in the Lower 48 has been so radically reshaped by petroleum as Oklahoma.

JAMES MCGIRK

Beneath its surface, Oklahoma is like an inverted mountain range. Oklahoma City floats on a pile of sedimentary rock more than 10,000 feet above the Cherokee shelf, a chasm of hard igneous "basement" rock that eventually slopes upwards to the northeast. "Oil and gas are formed by the alteration of microscopic organisms that have been deposited with sediment that turns into sedimentary rock," writes Oklahoma Geological Society's Dan T. Boyd. Beneath these billions of tons of rock, organic matter is squeezed until it comes apart on a molecular level and renders into short chains of carbon and hydrogen atoms (hence the name hydrocarbon). Any organic matter will do this given enough time and pressure, but usually the product diffuses irretrievably through the sedimentary rock above it. But not in a geological basin. (Or not as much.)

"Sediments and organic remains reach maximum thickness when they accumulate in large, gradually subsiding depressions called geological basins," writes Boyd. The oil becomes trapped between the lighter sedimentary rocks and the dense igneous rock, usually in plugs of dense brine, which act like cauls.

There are three major basins in Oklahoma: the Anadarko, Ardmore, and Arkoma basins, each a vast subterranean canyon complete with a trickle of oil and gas puddling at the bottom. Which is a fitting afterlife for Oklahoma's primordial organic matter, since this oil and gas were once plankton and other sundry underwater creatures.

For two hundred million years, according to David Baird and Danney Goble's *Oklahoma: A History*, the state lay submerged "beneath a shallow sea that, warmed by an equatorial sun, teemed with life." (Ecologically conscious readers will point out here that these critters spent hundreds of millions of years absorbing climate-changing carbon dioxide.) Over the next three hundred million years, the movement of tectonic plates—enormous slabs of rock floating on the earth's crust— jammed hills and mountains through the sea floor, or what was left of it since the water had long since drained away, and the squished sea-life percolated through a mile of light sedimentary rock and accumulated in an igneous trough and sat there unmolested until 1857, occasionally seeping to the surface.

PETRO STATE

People have always known about petroleum, particularly those who had a pyromaniacal streak. Phoenicians made smudge pots—crude, smoky lanterns—with the stuff, and it was probably one of the ingredients of Greek fire, a viscous fluid kind of like napalm the ancient Greeks would ignite and spray at enemy caravels. There were more mundane uses too, such as caulking baskets to make them waterproof, and for hallucinatory kicks: the Oracle of Delphi's portentous ravings may have come courtesy of natural gas seeping into her cave. Closer to home, when the first European explorers, trappers and frontiersmen, hacked their way through the Ozark Mountains and Cross Timbers they would keep an eye out for a telltale rainbow smear or a faint hiss and otherwise inexplicable paucity of plantlife. According to the Oklahoma Historical Society's website: "At Boyd Springs on Oil Creek in the Chickasaw Nation, travelers camping at the springs often drove a musket barrel into the water and ignited the seeping natural gas for illumination." Indian tribes, as famously depicted scooping oil-laced water from a creek by Charles Banks Wilson, would use it for medicine and magic. And the more anarchic types of frontiersmen would toss a match and run for cover, watching an entire river burst into flames.

Early prospectors were drawn to another product of Oklahoma's long-dead sea: its salt. And by 1859, about 20 years after the forced relocation of the Five Civilized Tribes, there were several commercial salt-drilling operations in the Indian territories. They were crude, often little more than pits lined with wooden planks with buckets to catch seeping salt water. Others were more sophisticated but dangerous, such as the spring pole—essentially a see-saw powered percussion drill, a sapling bent over a fulcrum, weighted down one side with a boulder, and the other, the bouncy side, driving a pole into the ground. Sometimes there was a steam engine powering the "downstroke," often in a configuration called the walking beam. But, more often than not, some poor flunky was tugging the other end of the spring pole up and down.

One day, a Cherokee salt-driller in Salina named Lewis Ross (brother of Chief John Ross, according to the American Oil and Gas Historical Society) noticed streaks of black ooze in his brine. He knew immediately what it was (after all, the first commercially successful oil well in the United States was drilled that year in Titusville, Pennsylvania), and he sold the ten barrels a year he produced as a cheap substitute for lamp

107

JAMES MCGIRK

fuel. Yet despite the growing demand for it, moving oil all the way from the Indian territories to big cities in the East (where it would be distilled and sold as kerosene and lubricant) was prohibitively expensive. As "oil fever" swept Pennsylvania and crude derricks and rickety wooden pipelines were erected out East, the price of crude sank. Then came the Civil War and the grueling, humiliating Reconstruction. It didn't seem worth drilling in faraway Oklahoma. The oil in the Indian territories was almost forgotten.

But not entirely. The Cherokee Nation began leasing concessions (a license for mineral rights) in 1884, and in 1889 Edward Byrd in the town of Chelsea in Rogers County drilled the first intentional Okie oil well. He found oil at 36 feet, according to the American Oil and Gas Historical Society, and his well produced half a barrel a day, which was "used as 'dip oil' to treat ticks." The secret was seeping out. And despite John D. Archbold's—the equivalent of chief operating officer in John D. Rockefeller's oil monopoly Standard Oil—notorious response to the suggestion of there being significant oil deposits in Oklahoma: "Are you crazy, man? Why, I'll drink every gallon of oil produced west of the Mississippi." Oil finders were beginning to snout around the Indian territories. John Galey, a Pennsylvania oil man who had found oil in Neodesha, Kansas, "got in his buggy and followed the mounds from Kansas to the mound at Bartlesville," where he met a man named George B. Keeler, who was running the Cherokee's general store.

"Mr. Galey said that he knew there was oil here because of the mounds which, in his opinion, had been thrown up by gas pressure," Keeler said. (Keeler himself had earlier noticed oil seeps near the Caney River.) Galey tried to lease land in Bartlesville, but the deal fell through after Galey heard about the enormous Spindletop well and headed south for Beaumont, Texas. Keeler and his partner William Johnstone decided to go it alone. They raised funds, hired a drilling company, and on April 15, 1897, gathered a crowd of spectators to watch "Keeler's stepdaughter, Jennie Cass, drop a go-devil (torpedo) down the shaft to set off a nitroglycerin charge [to shoot the well and loosen sand and rock to increase oil flow]," according to the Oklahoma Historical Society. Moments later the Nellie Johnstone No. 1 began flowing, becoming Oklahoma's first commercially successful well. Unfortunately this was too much oil for Oklahoma's budding market to bear, and the well was capped a few years later, poorly as it turned out. Oil spilled out and was accidentally set ablaze by ice-skaters on the Caney who'd lit a bonfire on the banks to keep warm. But more wells were opening, and in 1899 a rail-link to the refinery in Neodesha, Kansas, was completed, connecting Oklahoma's oil to the rest of the world. And then the really big Okie wells started coming online.

Between statehood and 1923, Oklahoma was America's largest oil-producing state, and even after it lost its perch to California and later Texas, Oklahoma still managed to increase its share of American output until 1929, when Oklahoma accounted for 750,000 barrels of oil a day and 35 percent of all the oil produced in the United States. Wells in Oklahoma City spat oil ferociously, so high that one out-of-control gusher—the Indian Territory Illuminating Oil Co.'s Mary Sudik No. 1, aka the "Wild Mary Sudik"—managed to sprinkle droplets on students in Norman, 11 miles away. Cushing alone produced 17 percent of American oil in 1919 and 3 percent of the world's output between 1912 and 1919. And all of this time there was plenty of appetite for new oil. The world's economy and its demand for petroleum and its distillates were increasing, and oil prices were holding steady for the most part, making Oklahoma's goliath output enormously profitable. Scores of millionaires were created. The Osage Nation managed to hold onto their mineral rights during the allotment phase. They charged oil companies a flat 10 percent royalty fee and paid each tribe member annual distributions equivalent to more than a million dollars today, which attracted scalawags and con men from all over the country eager to marry an Osage heir, which kicked off a string of killings that would come to be known as the Osage Reign of Terror. Meanwhile, the high wages paid by the oil industry led hundreds of thousands of former sharecroppers to descend on cities like Tulsa and Oklahoma City and the tiny boomtowns that would pop up whenever a new field was found. Oil money created architectural blooms and secondary and tertiary industries: engineering, manufacturing, insurance. There were counter-flows of capital and labor. Universities and colleges sprouted, which in turn revealed new methods of refining petroleum and natural gas. This stoked the economy even more.

JAMES McGIRK

And then the stock market collapsed, and oil prices—already under falling because of huge new discoveries in east Texas and Oklahoma—plunged. Texas and Oklahoma had a dilemma. They needed to restrict the supply of oil to keep the price of oil afloat (and preserve the fields for future), but individual oil producers had little incentive to choke off production because as prices came down they needed to pump a lot more to make the same amount of money.

Texas used its Railroad Commission and its charismatic commissioner, Ernest O. Thompson, to create a cartel system (which would eventually be used as a model for OPEC). The process was far from smooth in Texas, but it worked better than it did in Oklahoma. Oklahoma already had rules on its books about pro-rationing (these are mandatory production cuts during an oil glut), but Governor Murray wasn't quite as good at explaining them to his constituents as Commissioner Thompson was, and the Okie oilers revolted against him. Murray fought with his senate and declared martial law in the fields. He used the National Guard to shut productive wells and then called on the Guard again and again (sometimes for mundane tasks like collecting tolls or parking-ticket fines). Prices and production recovered after the Great Depression and crept up during World War II, which triggered another drilling boom, particularly as new technologies for scrying the earth (such as reading the reflected shockwaves from a dynamite detonation on a sonar array) were put to work. But this new wave ebbed in the 1960s when Middle Eastern oil flooded the system and prices fell once more. But prices picked up again after OPEC's oil embargo in the 1970s, and Okies rushed back to the fields, again armed with new technology, making new discoveries deep in the Anadarko Basin. Then the bottom dropped out of the market, and for 20 years Oklahoma's energy industry seemed to be dying out.

But the cycle has started again. Emerging markets like India and China have hoovered up all the excess capacity in the world's oil supply, and revolutions in the Middle East have shocked production and sent prices soaring. Oil prices are high (over $100 a barrel as I write this). And all of a sudden wells that were once considered too expensive or difficult to exploit are economically feasible.

PETRO STATE

There are two structures that define Oklahoma's relationship with energy today. Last year, the Devon Energy Corporation completed its new headquarters in Oklahoma City: a 50-story blazing glass behemoth that is easily the tallest skyscraper in Oklahoma. The thing cost nearly three-quarters of a billion dollars to build. It's a totem of corporate power, and in many ways reflects the company's investment in an extraordinary new technology—one that could make the United States a petroleum exporting country all over again. (Actually it does export oil, but has been a net importer of oil since 1967.)

The vast majority of petroleum isn't trapped in wells along the rims of geological basins but rather diffused in the sedimentary rock above it: the shale. For 20 years, a small engineering company called Mitchell Energy & Development Corp. had been trying to figure out how to release this potential bounty, even though gas prices were so low it hardly seemed worth it. In 1998 they figured it out; guided by 3-D seismic maps of subsurface geology, Mitchell Energy pioneered horizontal drilling and, as Daniel Yergin puts it in *The Quest*, "successfully adapted a fracking technique [hydraulic fracturing using a slurry of water and chemicals under high pressure to squeeze oil and gas out of wells]—what is known as LSF, or light sand fracking—to break up shale rock." George P. Mitchell, owner of Mitchell Energy, put his company up for sale—but with gas prices so low, no one was willing to buy. No one, that is, except for Devon Energy.

Mitchell's techniques—and the obscene price of oil—have unlocked huge reserves of shale oil in North America, the most famous being the oil sands in Alberta, Canada, and the Bakken Formation—an oily mass—stretching below the surfaces of Saskatchewan, Manitoba, Montana, and North Dakota. But getting the oil out of the ground is only the first step, there's also the herculean task of processing millions of barrels of oil a day and getting them to market. Which brings us almost all the way back to where we began.

Cushing, Oklahoma, ran out of oil of its own (in commercially viable quantities) long ago, but has become the center of America's crude oil distribution. For a long time this was more of an abstraction than anything else. Cushing was the place where West Texas Intermediate crude oil (this is the grade of American oil traded on the commodity market) was blended together and officially delivered. For most of its life Cushing

111

JAMES MCGIRK

sent Oklahoman, Texan, and Louisianan oil north to refineries in the Midwest, but now there's so much oil coming down from Canada and North Dakota that Cushing's traditional delivery points are full. Cushing is trying to retool itself to reverse the flow of oil and send northern oil down to refineries on the Gulf Coast. But they need new pipelines (such as the notorious Keystone XL), and the process of building them has been slow. Until they're finished there is a bit of a traffic jam in Cushing, causing a miniature glut of oil in the region that has actually driven the price of gasoline below what it should be, a fate reminiscent of the Nellie Johnstone No. 1 submerging Oklahoma's nascent oil market.

Surely you've noticed that the price of unleaded petrol in Tulsa has dipped below $3 a gallon. That's not necessarily good news for the Sooner state. The cycle of boom and bust may be about to tilt back into bust territory.

But that would only be temporary. The rush to develop new fields as gas prices rise and fall has long driven the oil and gas industry in Oklahoma, but perhaps there's another longer cycle operating beneath that. The most optimistic projections of the North American oil and gas sector suggest the United States could become a net exporter again by 2020. If this is true and Cushing is a harbinger and Oklahoma can maintain its position as the center of America's oil industry, perhaps we'll see another mad rush bloom of construction blossom in the Sooner state. Let's just hope the dire prognostications of climate change scientists don't come true—otherwise the second spurt of Oklahoma architecture could have to take place underwater.

SUBTERRANEAN PSYCHONAUT

The strange and dreadful saga of Gordon Todd Skinner, once the country's premier manufacturer of LSD

By *Michael Mason, Chris Sandel, and Lee Roy Chapman*

HE STOOD NAKED BY THE ROADSIDE with a blanket draped around his hips, feebly reaching out for the glimmering cars as they passed in the morning light. He was almost too hideous to look at: Purple and black tracks streaked across his frail limbs, and his hollow eyes peered out from a pale, gray head shaved bald, eyebrows and all. Brandon Andres Green was not from hell, not exactly. He was from Broken Arrow, Oklahoma.

Over the course of the past six days, Green had been tied up in a Tulsa hotel room, where his mind was loaded with powerful psychoactives and his body ravaged. He was then driven 500 miles south and abandoned in a Texas field at night. Green had crawled through the darkness, the occasional moan of a distant car his only guide. Every few feet, he collapsed from exhaustion. By morning, he reached the road. He grasped at fistfuls of air, hoping that someone might notice him.

It was 8:11 a.m. when Patrolman Neal Mora of the Texas City Police Department passed. He wasn't quite sure what he saw. He turned around, pulled over to the shoulder, then stepped out of his patrol car and approached the man cautiously.

"Help me, please," Green gasped.

The emergency techs showed up and loaded Green gingerly into the ambulance. They ran a few tests on his vitals. He had about 45 minutes left to live.

Green was no innocent, not back then. He was making a few hundred dollars a week selling weed and Ecstasy in Tulsa when he met the wrong girl, who introduced him to the wrong guy. He couldn't have known that he opened the gate to an underworld populated with federal agents, clandestine chemistry, and mystical orders. A world in which one man, Gordon Todd Skinner, felt at home.

It was April of 2003 when Green—18 at the time, still grinding out his final semester of high school—first laid eyes on Krystle Cole. She was the cute blonde in pigtails at a South Tulsa rave offering Ecstasy to Green's friends. Green eyed her baggy pants, her form under a fitted t-shirt. He asked her to meet him in the hall, to see if he could buy 50 pills. He was a dealer too, he explained. She patted Green down, probing him with questions. He thought her paranoia was cute. Cole said she'd call him soon to negotiate a deal, and she did, around noon the next day.

They met at a Burger King near the University of Tulsa. Cole handed Green an envelope, then asked him for his car keys. Green waited inside while Cole searched his car. Wait 30 minutes before opening the envelope, Cole said. Inside were directions to a nearby Taco Bell, where Green found a note addressed to him hidden in the ladies' room. Green saw a tall, bearded man in the parking lot, a guy he noticed at the rave the night before. The notes led Green to a pay phone in a sandwich shop, then a call led to the nearby Peace of Mind bookstore, where he found a final message hidden in a specific book that instructed him to meet Cole in the parking lot of a health food store.

The game took hours, ending with Cole inviting Green into her car. It was time to meet her chemist friend. Green saw the balding, bearded man—the same from the rave and from the Taco Bell parking lot—parked nearby. The man said he knew how to cook all sorts of drugs, and that he'd been involved in serious deals since he was a teenager; that he'd been all over the world, met with insiders, and even served a little time. And now he was looking for some help. Would Green be interested in some real work, a gig that involved a kilo of LSD in Amsterdam? Cole made the introduction: Brandon, meet Gordon Todd Skinner.

Around Skinner, Green felt intoxicated. At the time, Green was a senior at Victory Christian School—a pretty boy, slight of build with long, golden hair and blue eyes. He was naïve and easily entertained, the kind of guy who would get fruited to the gills at raves. Skinner was everything Green was not: big, strong, hyper-intelligent, worldly, and otherworldly. Green needed to get a legitimate job to distract the authorities, they told him. He would need to abandon the party scene for a discrete, seemingly ordinary life. If everything went well, and Green proved himself to be a talented understudy, then they could talk about the transaction in Amsterdam. It could bring in millions. Green was excited, and terrified. Skinner and Cole were grooming Green to be a better drug dealer. Just the week before he bought a fake Mazzio's Pizza uniform to fool his parents into thinking he had an after-school job. Now two accomplished drug traffickers clamored to mentor him. He never heard of Gordon Todd Skinner or Krystle Cole before.

"You realize you're in too deep to back out now," Skinner told Green.

During his high school years in the early 1980s, Gordon Todd Skinner often showed up to Cascia Hall Preparatory School in his blue blazer, with the school crest proudly emblazoned on his chest. On free dress days, he wore a karate gi, or sometimes a tux, to school. A classmate of Skinner's recalls seeing him arrive in a 1957 Bentley S1. He wore a full-length camel-hair coat.

A tall, fleshy math geek, Skinner didn't play sports like football or basketball. Instead, he dominated at chess.

"I played him one afternoon and beat him," the classmate remembered. "But as the game drew closer to a conclusion, and Skinner realized he would certainly lose, he began taunting me for not finishing him off quickly enough. He said my finishing game was weak. That's just the type of guy Gordon Todd Skinner was. He always had to be in control of the situation. Even when he really wasn't."

Chess was a longstanding passion, but by the age of 15, Skinner discovered another obsession: drugs, and everything related. At 16, he could extract psychedelic tryptamines from plant life. He offered them to friends.

"All of my high school friends just lined up to take anything that I had, and it was—they were volunteering, so it wasn't a problem," Skinner says, fanning his fingers over the cafeteria table in Joseph Harp Correctional Center in Lexington, Oklahoma, a world and a life away from his Tulsa prep school. His hair is mostly gray now, the crown of his head smooth as a cremini's cap.

Skinner's mother, a Tulsa business woman named Katherine Magrini, married Gary Lee Magrini. Skinner's stepfather was a special criminal agent with the U.S. Treasury Department, which, at the time, handled scores of drug investigations. Federal agents visited the Magrini home regularly. From an early age, Skinner learned that he could dabble in the world of drugs right under the government's nose. Either nobody cared, or nobody noticed.

Skinner tried stronger drugs on his friends, studying them like insects. He was known to bring a tank of nitrous oxide to school so he and his pals could inhale in the bathroom between classes. One weekend, according to a classmate, Skinner experimented on another student, dosing him heavily with something he'd conjured. The teen was later found in front of a full-length mirror, naked and talking to his reflection. He tried to negotiate a cocaine deal with an oak tree.

"I was just a scientist saying, 'Try this out.' And unfortunately, they were all just guinea pigs in line," Skinner recalls. "Some of them thought it was great, and some of them don't talk to me to this day over it."

Religion and psychedelics enjoy a marriage over millennia. One of the most evocative myths pertains to Soma, or Chandra, the havoc-creating moon lord of plants in Vedic Brahmanism. "Let Indra drink, O Soma, of thy juice for wisdom," the *Rig Veda* proclaims. The ethnomycologist R. Gordon Wasson equated Soma with the psychedelic mushroom *Amanita muscaria*, the same mushroom that appears in Siberian folklore and ancient Central American pottery. The use of mushrooms, fungi, and other plant-related hallucinogens permeate indigenous spiritual traditions, but it wasn't until 1938 that a Swiss scientist, Albert Hofmann, tried synthesizing ergotamine (an extract of ergot fungi) and wound up

SUBTERRANEAN PSYCHONAUT

with lysergic acid diethylamide, or LSD. Reports quickly spread about its mind-altering effects. Even the U.S. government was curious.

Dr. Frank Olson, a biological warfare specialist, stayed at the Hotel Statler in New York City. Unbeknownst to him, the Central Intelligence Agency dosed him with enough LSD to seriously impair his mental state. On Saturday, November 28, 1953, Olson's trip ended when he was pushed from, thrown out, or jumped out of the glass window of his room and plummeted 10 floors down. *The Frederick News-Post* said Olson was depressed and complained of ulcers. Today, we know his death was the result of a covert CIA project known as MK-ULTRA, which dosed unwitting men, women, and children with LSD for scientific research. The program was declassified in 2001, but nobody knows how many died as a result of the experimentation. Olson's family settled with the U.S. government for $750,000.

The CIA's drug experimentation projects took root post-WWII. Initially they focused on discovering new techniques for mind control, torture, and brainwashing. Similar CIA projects grew in scope and ambition during the 1950s, and included subjects like future counterculture figures such as Ken Kesey, Robert Hunter, and Ted Kaczynski. In his book *The Electric Kool-Aid Acid Test*, Tom Wolfe documented the transition of LSD into American mainstream culture. By the late 1960s, LSD was on the tips of myriad tongues, with about 20,000 being introduced to the drug annually.

In 1966, a gang of sophisticated, elusive peacenik drug smugglers called "The Brotherhood of Eternal Love" became a prolific supplier of LSD stateside and to soldiers fighting the Vietnam War. Using a retail front called Mystic Arts World in Laguna Beach, California, the Brotherhood began its crusade to deliver LSD to the masses, for the purpose of spiritual enlightenment. Under their auspices, the ingenious chemist Nick Sand produced 3.6 million hits of acid in 1969. His product "Orange Sunshine" was the most popular form of LSD of all time.

When core members of The Brotherhood of Eternal Love were busted in August of 1972, Nick Sand was among those whose futures were blotted. Rumor had it that a bright, young trust-fund kid named Leonard Pickard, also an aspiring chemist, donated to Sand's legal battle.[1]

---

1. Journalist Dan Casey of the *Roanoke Times* claims to know Sand. Casey says Sand told him Pickard had contributed to Sand's defense. Pickard claims he is not personally acquainted with Sand and did not contribute to either his 1973 or 1996 proceedings.

MASON, SANDEL, AND CHAPMAN

In 1976, Sand was convicted and sentenced to 15 years. He appealed his case on the technicality that he actually produced a close variant of LSD called ALD-52, which was legal at the time. Sand was released on a $50,000 bail and disappeared into the ether. Two years later, Pickard, then a student at Stanford, was charged with attempting to manufacture a controlled substance.[2]

In the mid-to-late '70s, LSD production was interrupted by law enforcement. Availability remained comparably low for the next 30 years. The controlled substance was, it seemed, under control. Cocaine-fueled hustlers discoed across illuminated dance floors, Elvis left the building with 14 different compounds in his body, and Nancy Reagan coached children to "Just Say No." Meanwhile, across the desert, in the middle of the country, a new maestro of the underground drug industry was loosed upon the land.

_____

While Skinner lab-ratted his pals at Cascia Hall, at home he was submerged in a federal alphabet soup. Skinner's stepfather, Magrini, earned an appointment as criminal enforcement agent for the Internal Revenue Service,[3] and the front door of the Magrini house, according to Skinner, revolved with the constant stream of G-men from the FBI, DEA, IRS, and CBP.[4] Many of them were soldiers in the War on Drugs, a governmental prohibition campaign that was coined by President Richard Nixon and escalated by President Ronald Reagan. In 1986, Congress passed the Anti-Drug Abuse Act, which poured an additional $1.7 billion into funding the War on Drugs.

"They all came to our house and ate at our parties—I grew up with these guys. They talked shop non-stop," says Skinner, calling from prison

_____

2. Regarding the case, Pickard writes: "The 1976 charge: the defense position was that the lab equipment was derived a job repairing same at a recycling firm. I was held 4-1/2years without a plea, then released on the same day in exchange for said plea, in this instance, *nolo contendere*, or no contest. The time served was the maximum under California state law, minus good time."

3. According to Skinner, Magrini was later assigned to the IRS as a special agent. According to freepickardonline.org, Magrini was assigned to the DEA in 1984.

4. Federal Bureau of Investigation, Drug Enforcement Agency, Internal Revenue Service, and U.S. Customs and Border Patrol.

now. "The FBI guys would ask me to look into stuff for them, and I did this on a regular basis."

Skinner is serving life plus 90 years for kidnapping-related charges. His cellmates refer to him as Dr. Lecter. He distrusts the FBI more than any other agency, and warns that the line is being monitored and that it might be blocked, because "that's how they do me here."

Skinner's ties to a number of other government agencies deepened in step with his drug experimentation repertoire. He didn't really enjoy marijuana or other common drugs, but gravitated toward entheogens, the sorts of drugs that shamans and other spiritualists use. He read most every book he could find on the matter. One of his favorite libraries was Peace of Mind bookstore in Tulsa. Barry Bilder, the owner, became a longtime friend to Skinner.

"When I met him, Todd was still in high school," Bilder said. "He would come in and buy all these drug books, and he had a tremendous collection that he bought over a period of years."

During his early years of studying, Skinner didn't involve himself in his experiments with psychedelics, preferring to observe their effects on his classmates and friends. Later, he started the journey within.

"I was a little nervous messing with the neurocomplex of the mind," Skinner once explained to a courtroom.

At around 19, Skinner was ready to step into the fairy ring. He had acquired 10,000 peyote buttons on behalf of a Native American church and extracted a variety of alkaloids from the supply. He decided he would take the synthesized mescaline.

"It was profound," Skinner says. "That's all I can tell you... I saw colors, and I was in a room that was small and all of a sudden it was like a set on the Ponderosa."

Skinner then decided to push the experience further. He fasted for two weeks, then consumed 52 peyote buttons.

"I rolled over and I could just see all the stars and it was amazing," Skinner says, smiling up at the fluorescent lights. "I had what I'd call a peak experience—and I'd call it religious because you become instantly connected with everything in the universe. That was a turning point for me. I was a scientist prior to that."

MASON, SANDEL, AND CHAPMAN

In the natural camp of entheogens, you've got peyote, psilocybin mushrooms, salvia, and ayahuasca, to name a few; LSD, MDMA,[5] and 2C-B are synthetic. Then there's Todd Skinner's catalog, a menagerie of exotic entheogens that requires the help of a chemist to decipher. When Skinner took the stand in January 2003, the judge asked him what drugs he had used. Skinner replied:

> I would like to start with the ones I don't use. I never used, to the best of my knowledge, any form of tobacco plant. I never used methamphetamine. Never used cocaine... I have not used street drugs in general. I have avoided most street drugs. I've not used PCP. The reason I'm doing the 'nots' is because I've done so many unusual analogues that the list gets to be long.

According to a list he provided to the courts, the number of all the drugs he ingested, inhaled, injected, inserted, snorted, or otherwise introduced into his body comes to 163, and is much higher when counting the derivatives of certain substances. When Skinner elaborated on a particular drug, he conveyed the sort of obsession you'd expect from a vintner.

> I went through an elaborate process and consumed ibotenic acid, which would have been the active constituent. I rarely did this. I was nervous about the research, because of the decarboxylation of ibotenic acid that converts to muscimol, which is an active constituent of fly agaric or *Amanita muscaria*.

Skinner can wax poetic on PCP-A receptors and the differences between pharmahuascas and 5-fluoro-alpha-methyltryptamine, but when the judge finally asked Skinner why he wanted to use entheogens, Skinner went flush.

---

5. Psychonauts split hairs, arguing that Ecstasy [MDMA] is actually an empathogen, which enhances feelings of oneness between people rather than between the self and the universe.

Subterranean Psychonaut

> I seem to have an idiosyncratic response to entheogens, that they are—have—maybe that's arrogant, so I've got to be careful. They are very spiritual and sacramental things. I do not use these—I think you put it "recreationally," and I take offense to that, unfortunately, because I do not take these things recreationally. These are sacraments to me.

To achieve such a communion, Skinner employed a concoction of pyschoactives he called "The Eucharist": a communion wafer laced with a panoply of lysergamides ranging from ALD-52 to extract of morning glory seeds, with a sip of ergot wine. Skinner conducted the ceremonies with "the sacrament," and regularly administered the rite before large congregations of friends.

Numerous accounts from Skinner's associates describe seeing Skinner act in a priestly manner, conferring the hallucinogenic host upon eager tongues and offering a chalice to waiting lips. Within half an hour, his sheep met god. Or the devil.

"A lot of people, when they met Todd at his highest, they would say something to me like, 'Barry, that guy is the Buddha,' " Bilder said. "But what I'm suggesting is that Todd had something in his being, this thing that wasn't right. He had made a pact early on in his life, maybe it was even in previous existences, where he said, 'This is what I'm gonna do: I'm going to be here to create havoc.' "

On the witness stand in 2003, Gordon Todd Skinner was 39 years old and speaking like a priest of Soma.[6] But earlier in his spiritual journey, Skinner was seduced into another underworld, one of unholy adventures, a world where drugs were both faith and works. As a young man, Skinner partook in the most secretive of all arts. He became a government informant.

---

6. From "Soma," by Stephen Naylor in *Encyclopedia Mythica*: "Though he is never depicted in human form, Soma obviously did not want for lovers; poets rarely do. In one episode, his desires caused a war. He had grown arrogant due to the glory that was offered him. Because of this, he let his lust overcome him; he kidnapped and carried off Tara, the wife of the god Bri-haspati. After refusing to give her up, the gods made war on him to force her release, and Soma called on the asuras to aid him. Finally Brahma interceded and compelled Soma to let Tara go. But she was with child, and it ended up that this child was Soma's. The child was born and named Budha (not to be confused with the Buddha)."

Skinner's first notable case came in 1983 by way of a money-laundering scheme; he initiated the case by calling Agent McLean with the FBI. In a later and more significant operation, Skinner helped HIDTA, High Intensity Drug Trafficking Area, Group #2 out of Florida (primarily managed by CBP), set up a complex sting operation with a man named Boris Olarte who was in the federal witness protection program.[7] In 1989, Olarte was then used to extradite and arrest José Rafael Abello Silva, a Columbian cocaine smuggler. His arrest contributed to the downfall of the Medellín drug cartel. As he informed, Skinner gathered intelligence on how government agencies dealt with drugs. Work as an informant turned out to be great training for a person interested in the trade, but it wasn't enough to help Skinner avoid prosecution.

Earlier that year, Skinner was arrested and jailed in New Jersey for distribution of marijuana. Skinner's bail was set at one million dollars. While serving time, he met fellow inmate William Hauck, who was incarcerated for a sex offense.[8] Through the '90s, Hauck surfaced intermittently in Skinner's life, usually as a truck driver for Katherine Magrini's company, but sometimes as an accessory to Skinner's drug-related transactions. Skinner and Hauck were never really friends, perhaps because Skinner suspected Hauck of having longstanding ties to government agencies. Skinner's suspicions remained benign, until Hauck figured much larger in Skinner's life.

THE SILO TESTIMONIES

Todd Skinner wasn't just a psychedelic spiritualist, nor was he merely a government informant. He was business-minded, and he understood the high demand for entheogens. If he could just find the right chemist—someone who knew how to set up a sophisticated lab where LSD could be produced—the possibilities and the profits were boundless. Alfred Savinelli,

---

7. Around 1987, Skinner's mother, Katherine Magrini, owned a candy shop where she sold a delectable she called "Okie Power." She was reported to have sold this enterprise to Boris Olarte. According to Leonard Pickard's timeline, Olarte's wife, Clara Lacle, was residing with Magrini. Lacle flew to Aruba with FBI agents to set up Olarte's supplier Abello Silva.

8. According to a DEA report dated 7/31/2003, Hauck stated he had been jailed for having sex with his 17-year-old sister-in-law. He was charged in December of 1989 for a criminal sexual act in New Jersey.

a friend of Skinner's and part of the entheogen community, recalls when Skinner asked him if he knew where he could meet an elusive, gifted chemist named Leonard Pickard. Rumor had it Pickard was advancing the field of LSD chemistry. Savinelli knew Pickard. He felt Skinner's ambition and Pickard's naïveté would make a disastrous combination. Salvinelli shrugged Skinner off.

Pickard was still around, just not very visible. After serving time in the '70s for possession and manufacturing, Pickard seemingly vanished from the scene, until he was jailed in the late '80s. He did five years for manufacturing. Later, word got around that Pickard was in the DEA's pocket.

Throughout the 1990s, Pickard continued moving in hallucinogenic circles. While taking classes at UC Berkeley, Pickard attended a series of potlucks—dinner conversations that centered on consciousness studies. He lived in a Zen center, earned a master's degree from Harvard, and studied the migration of LSD use. Late in the decade, his associates claimed to see the professorial Pickard dealing with large amounts of loot. Pickard explained away any secretive behavior as related to his work for the FBI, DEA, and other agencies.

The similarities between Pickard and Skinner were extensive: both were entheogen enthusiasts, capable clandestine chemists, lawbreakers, and informants for the government. When they met each other at the 1997 Entheobotany Shamanic Plant Science Conference[9] in San Francisco, it was as though their convergence were ordained by a fungal power.

"When I met him, [Skinner] was using exotic structures every week or every few days," Pickard told *Rolling Stone*. "He loved to eat ayahuasca and its various analogues."

Pickard says that Skinner was offering research grants at the conference, which piqued his pockets.

---

9. Throughout the literature on Pickard and Skinner, this conference is often mistakenly referred to as an "ethnobotony" conference. An article from the *San Francisco Chronicle* indicates that this conference is the first time Skinner and Pickard met. Pickard's timeline suggests that they met later, in February 1998, at a chance encounter in a San Francisco hotel lobby where the chemist Alexander "Sasha" Shulgin was speaking. Skinner claims that Pickard was wheeling around $700K in cash in his luggage bag at the time, claiming he was being followed.

"Basically I just made up quite a story to [Pickard] and told him that we could possibly get some money from [billionaire Warren] Buffett," Skinner later revealed on the witness stand. "And I had quite a bit of fun with that one, but it really, in the end, upset him quite a bit."

Pickard and Skinner met several times at Skinner's house in Stinton, California (its former occupant was Jerry Garcia). It was a party pad frequented by insiders of the entheogen world and the perfect place for Pickard and Skinner to talk business.

Just a year earlier, Skinner had acquired an Atlas-E missile silo at 16795 Say Road in Wamego, Kansas. He lived there and planned to use it as a facility for his mother's industrial manufacturing company, Gardner Spring Incorporated. As a home, it provided Skinner two of the things he valued immensely: seclusion and privacy.

The missile silo was the ultimate Skinner Box. He renovated the military complex, adding a luxury sound system and a group-sized hot tub. Llamas and Clydesdale horses roamed above ground while pretty girls and hardcore partiers voyaged to chemical wonderlands below.[10] Skinner's silo became a vortex of local gossip, with stories and rumors that continue to percolate about Wamego to this day.

Legends of Pickard and Skinner's partnership circulated the globe and remain debated in countless online forums. *Rolling Stone* magazine presented Pickard's account of the silo years in their 2001 article "The Acid King," which portrayed Skinner as a Kurtz-like con man whose ghoulish escapades into experimentation culminate with the fatal overdose of a friend in April of 1999. Skinner's version of events, however, differs from Pickard's.

---

10. "I had two Clydesdales, three miniature horses, one miniature donkey," Skinner told a courtroom. "And the llama herd expanded and contracted over time, so I can't give you an exact number of hoofed, even though they would not be classified, quote, hoofed animals, the llamas, but let's say between two and eight."

SKINNER'S RECOLLECTION

Skinner testified that he and Pickard mapped out a working business and started a clandestine lab at a house in Aspen, Colorado. That location wasn't an ideal chemical processing facility, though. The house was in bad condition, which meant a continual parade of plumbers and carpenters. That, plus high rent and chemical spills sent Pickard and Skinner packing to Santa Fe, likely in late '98 or early '99. Turned out the move was smart financially.

When Judge Richard Roberts of Topeka, Kansas, asked Skinner how much LSD was being made and how often during the Santa Fe LSD operation, Skinner couldn't answer him exactly. He wasn't there often enough during the manufacturing process to know volume, he said. Skinner says he did manage cash flow from a West Coast figure named "Petaluma Al," and estimated that within one year's time the Santa Fe operation generated about $30 million dollars in revenue—roughly enough acid to send all of Spain and France tripping.

The problem with a successful LSD lab is that it can attract attention, and then all those boxes of tax-free, dirty money create paranoia.[11] It's unwise to operate out of the same place for more than two years, which is why Pickard, Clyde Apperson (their set-up and takedown guy), and Skinner went prospecting in Kansas. They looked at an Atlas-F missile silo near Salina, Kansas—a short drive from Skinner's own Atlas-E silo (the main difference between the two types of silos is that Atlas-F missiles were stored vertically, while Atlas-E were horizontal). They couldn't use Skinner's silo because the property's paperwork had Skinner's name all over it, making it susceptible to close investigation. By this point, the government was keeping tabs on Skinner at the Wamego base, but the Atlas-F silo had certain features that made government intrusion nearly impossible.

---

11. Skinner claimed he kept a group of lower-level staff who would exchange moneys at casinos and elsewhere. One of the operation's logistical strategies involved unloading huge volumes of Dutch guilders into the Las Vegas market—a tricky feat, as the guilder was simultaneously depreciating. Pickard and Skinner were moving so much cash at the time, Skinner says, that they wouldn't bother to account for transactions under $30,000. He says they refused to use any bills less than $20 on the grounds, that lesser currency took up too much space.

MASON, SANDEL, AND CHAPMAN

"[There were] Very little above-ground ways of doing observation—a heavy-duty structure to where it would be harder to break into and with lots of space being around it and a military fence..." Skinner recalled from the stand during Pickard's trial. "You would be able to tell if you were under surveillance."

Tim Schwartz owned the Atlas-F silo. Schwartz was the property dealer who sold Skinner the silo in Wamego. Skinner told Schwartz he was interested in using the Atlas-F, so Schwartz struck an informal agreement with Skinner that allowed him to use the Atlas-F base while Schwartz was traveling the country. Skinner claimed that not long after, around December of 1999, he, Pickard, and Apperson began using the Atlas-F missile base for their LSD operation. It was the Wamego missile base, however, that began to wave a red flag.

With the successful setup at the Atlas-F base, the first months of the new millennium held a promise of unprecedented profits from drug trafficking. That's when a balding and bearded Gordon Todd Skinner first met Krystle Cole at a Topeka gentlemen's club, where she was an 18-year-old pigtailed stripper who performed a country-girl-gone-bad routine. When she saw Skinner enter the club, Cole remembers thinking to herself, "What a sick-o! Did Amish men really go into strip clubs? Weird!" But then they fell into a deep conversation. Soon, Skinner convinced Cole to join him at his missile base.

Cole and Skinner were the sort of soulmates who shared the same order of the same genus of the same species. In the dank innards of Skinner's silo, their viscid bodies fused over LSD and Ecstasy trips. They experimented with hallucinogenic suppositories.

"We knew how deeply we loved each other," Cole recalls in her exclamation-heavy 2007 book *Lysergic,* which she claims has been optioned for film production. "No questions. The deepest love ever, a sacred love. We worshiped each other as divine interlocking pieces of god."

In one cinematic chapter, Cole and Skinner meet up with a suave Pickard and his Russian fiancée, Natasha. The four enjoyed a high-rolling, free-loving weekend in Las Vegas.

Within three years of starting their romance, Skinner and Cole will participate in a blood-dripping, vomit-spewing incident that will end with kidnapping charges for both of them.

VICE magazine's short documentary "High on Krystle" offers a peek into the life of Skinner's comrade in expanded consciousness. During the video, the cosmic Cole takes the host, Hamilton Morris, on a giggly tour of the Wamego missile base. She explains how the corrugated, cylindrical corridors "are really fun when you're tripping, because they'll start swirling on you."

Cole left a detail out of *Lysergic*'s love story: Skinner's other love. Around 1997, he started dating a woman named Emily Ragan. When Skinner met Cole at the strip club, it wasn't a random encounter—he was interviewing her for a job as his personal assistant.

"Krystle was a great valet," he remembers, adding, "She was very well organized."

At the same time Cole was finding herself enmeshed with Skinner's soul, Skinner was growing closer to Ragan as well. In September of 2000, Skinner married Ragan. They had a daughter together, and divorced the following year. Through her current husband, Ragan declined to comment for this story. Skinner says he eventually fell in love with Cole.

While Skinner's testimony during the Pickard trial depicted an industrious atmosphere at the silo, Cole had a different take, likening the milieu to that of an entheogenic monastery. Cole recalls lots of nudity and wild parties where people used IVs to blast themselves into deliria. Somewhere in the subterranean haze, Krystle recalled a ritual in which Skinner initiated her into an order using a golden chalice, ergot wine, and ancient Chaldean prayers. In *Lysergic*, she theorizes that the Last Supper might have been similarly infested.

"Doesn't this seem a little like the communion of Christianity?" Cole asks.

Depressed and recently divorced, Tim Schwartz, the Atlas-F's property owner, committed suicide in March of 2000. Someone was bound to reclaim the silo soon. Schwartz's father finally contacted Skinner in July and asked him to immediately move out any belongings and to remove the locks. Both Apperson and Pickard were away at the time, so Skinner made the only choice he could: He gathered a few trusted friends and moved the entire lab, chemicals and all, out of the Atlas-F

MASON, SANDEL, AND CHAPMAN

silo and into his Atlas-E residence in Wamego.[12] Fearing Pickard and Apperson's fury, Skinner lied and told them that he had moved the lab to a facility near Topeka.

The LSD operation, in Skinner's mind, was untenable. He questioned Pickard's integrity, and felt as though the entire effort was polluted by corruption and greed. Worst of all, he suspected that Pickard may have been involved in the murder of an informant.[13] Around August of 2000, he expressed to Krystle Cole and others that he was going to inform on Pickard. In a later meeting with Pickard in California, Skinner explained that he was planning to marry Emily Ragan and would return the lab equipment soon thereafter.

The DEA's silo investigation, "Operation White Rabbit," began in October 2000, when Skinner decided to approach the government as an informant. In the weeks that followed, Skinner took DEA agents into the Wamego silo under the guise of giving a property tour, and he recorded calls he made to Pickard.

On November 6, 2000, Clyde Apperson pulled his Ryder truck out of the Wamego missile silo property. Inside was some of the LSD lab equipment they had reclaimed from the Atlas-E silo grounds, along with a small amount of precursor.[14] Pickard trailed Apperson in a Buick LeSabre. They hadn't made it far before their caravan was pulled over by the Kansas Highway Patrol. Pickard, a marathon runner, took off

---

12. Skinner's account of moving the lab is dramatic: He calls Pickard in London who warns him not to move the lab, and Pickard even says he's taking the next flight in. Skinner tells him there's no time. He rounds up several friends, along with his biological father, Gordon H. Skinner, to retrieve the equipment. When they enter the silo, they discover that the lab is in shocking condition: it has standing water in it, with electrical cords and toxic trash floating in the area. The chemical odor was powerful, yet the group still risked heavy exposure to dangerous chemicals in order to move the lab. One friend, Gunner Guinan, was heavily exposed to LSD, and Skinner said that there were "32 to 36 hours of not being able to communicate with him." All in all, it took three days to disassemble and move the lab. Skinner returned the keys to the Atlas-F silo with three hours to spare. Clyde Apperson showed up soon thereafter, claiming he was in the hospital with a viral ear infection and agreed that Skinner had needed to move the lab.
13. Skinner says that federal agents later told him the informant had not been killed after all.
14. Later, the DEA learned that the precursor that was found at the silo was ergocristine, which was then uncontrolled.

running into the cold Kansas fields, only to be found by a farmer and arrested a day later.

During the ensuing trial, Pickard's worst suspicions were confirmed. Skinner had signed the DEA's Confidential Source Agreement form. It offered some level of immunity, but not enough to make him feel safe. On October 19, the Department of Justice struck a deal with Skinner, offering him an incredibly broad umbrella of protection in a letter that stated:

> In exchange for your agreement to cooperate with the undersigned and/or other federal agents, the United States Department of Justice, Narcotic and Dangerous Drug Section agrees that no statement or other information (including documents) given by you during this and subsequent meetings will be used directly or indirectly against you in any criminal case...

Skinner was ready to spill, an act commemorated in a 706-page document called *The Transcript of the Testimony of Gordon Todd Skinner Had Before Honorable Richard D. Rogers and a Jury of 12 on January 28, 2003.*

"How is cooperation such as you're doing viewed in that [drug] community?" the judge asked Skinner.

"In certain segments, this is the death penalty," Skinner replied.

Skinner's reasoning involved more than just saving himself legally, he claims; it was an indictment of his own character. He was a product of a Catholic private school, a man who was willing to testify against his own partners in an illegal-drug enterprise, and an ambitious businessman. He explained it this way:

> I was a member of a system [the Brotherhood], the whole entire lineage of the sacraments were contaminated fundamentally," he told the court. "This was an absolute violation at the highest level of an organization of a spiritual means, even though the deeper I looked into this organization, the more corrupt I found it to be. And even the corruption was on myself.

MASON, SANDEL, AND CHAPMAN

When Pickard had a chance to counter Skinner's testimony, his story was a wholesale refutation of Skinner's account. The Santa Fe operation never existed as such, Pickard claimed. Instead, it was a lab established by Skinner to manufacture ayahuasca. He claimed only incidental contact with Skinner until late 1999, and after that point, "perhaps a dinner each month" until Pickard's arrest in Kansas. Skinner's entire testimony was essentially another one of Skinner's elaborate con games, Pickard thought, one in which Pickard was merely the patsy.

"Many other individuals have been the victims of [Skinner's] grifting, unwitting of his actual background," Pickard wrote in a recent email. "He has the capacity to weave convincing fictions about others, both real persons and imaginary ones, and extend these confabulations for days in the greatest detail."

But a slew of witness testimonies also appeared inconsistent with Pickard's defense. Alfred Savinelli, who provided some of the lab equipment, said that Pickard made him worry for his own safety and that of his family.[15] Another man, David Haley, claimed that Pickard had paid him $300,000 to lease a house in Santa Fe for a two-year period. DEA Agent Karl Nichols offered a number of phone records and financial transactions that provoked suspicion.

On November 25, 2003, Leonard Pickard and Clyde Apperson were found guilty of conspiring to manufacture, distribute, and dispense 10 grams or more of a "mixture" or a substance containing a detectable amount of LSD. But if not for his arrangement with the government, Gordon Todd Skinner might have stood with them. In a 2004 statement by DEA Administrator Karen P. Tandy:

> DEA dismantled the world's leading LSD manufacturing organization headed by William Leonard Pickard. This was the single largest seizure of an operable LSD lab in DEA's history. On November 6, 2000, DEA agents seized from an abandoned missile silo located near Wamego, Kansas, approximately 91 pounds of LSD, 215 pounds of lysergic acid (an LSD precursor chemical), 52 pounds of iso-LSD

---

15. At a coffee shop, Savinelli received a note that he perceived as a death threat, and he surmised that note came from or through Pickard.

SUBTERRANEAN PSYCHONAUT

(an LSD manufacturing by-product), and 42 pounds of ergocristine... Since that operation, reported LSD availability declined by 95 percent nationwide.

The press release was hyperbolic. The DEA reportedly captured 91 pounds of a substance that contained minute amounts of LSD. Testimony suggested the presence of only an estimated seven ounces of LSD. If Skinner or Pickard produced or stockpiled a larger amount of LSD, it had essentially vanished from the DEA's grasp.[16]

Pickard is serving two life sentences. Apperson received 30 years. Skinner walked. The entheogen community, which was just gaining ground with legitimate research and studies, fell apart.

"It was torpedoed," recalls Savinelli. "Everybody dug in deep and disappeared and sought protection. I've stayed away from most of my friends for a decade."

LIFE OUT OF THE SILO

In early 2003, a chapter of life closed on Gordon Todd Skinner. In the eyes of some, he was an enlightened spiritualist, a demonic criminal, a brilliant businessman, or a gifted liar. The spiritual community that he once prized was obliterated, he had turned on his business partners and ruined an empire, his health began to fail him, and the heat from government agencies surrounded him.

"I was in a really good mood," Skinner says. "I know you'd have a hard time believing that, but I was under enormous stress prior to the trial... When I got off the stand and I was released by the judge, I was one happy dude—I was ready to leave the United States."

Skinner's high spirits would not last long. They flew out the door, along with Krystle Cole.

Cole first realized she loved Todd Skinner in Las Vegas, the same place she claimed to party with Pickard. But that was 2000, and now, in

---

16. During a tour of the Wamego missile silo, the current owner stated that in 2006, someone broke into the silo, tore through some specific tiles in one of the bathrooms, and reclaimed "who knows what" from the hiding spot.

2003, she had a supplemental love: the 18-year-old drug dealer Brandon Green. Cole, the older woman at 21, stood before a mirror in her hotel room. Green watched her practice an "I'm just a small-town girl" alibi, the same one she'd rehearsed every night of their romantic getaway. She had the alibi down solid.

Cole and Green had escaped from Skinner because they feared him. When they first met, Skinner and Green bonded over their love of drugs and travel. They told each other about their favorite trips (the literal ones, including destinations like the Netherlands and Germany). Initially, Green suspected that Cole's relationship with Skinner wasn't anything traditional, and in time, it became apparent to him that they weren't exclusive to one another at all. Green cultivated a fondness for Cole, and she for him. At first, Skinner acted as if he wasn't affected by the intimacy between the two. But then, by late spring of 2003, Green noticed that Skinner's demeanor changed. He slept less and lost a significant amount of weight. He grew disheveled and unkempt. Skinner was under inevitable stress as the Pickard trial progressed in a Kansas courtroom, his enterprise with Pickard had ground to a halt, and he was more than just a bright dot on the law enforcement radar screen.

One night, Skinner showed up at Green's apartment while he was away, took Cole from the living room by force, and then sped away with her. Cole claimed Skinner had threatened to drive off a bridge.

"Todd has an anger about him that is very scary," recalls Green, who sounds a little nervous. "You know when his face turns red—and he is a big guy. He just seems crazy. You don't want to piss him off." It's a quiet afternoon at a restaurant in Norman, Oklahoma, near Green's home. It's been 10 years since the kidnapping, and this is the first time he's ever told his side in its entirety.

That incident shocked Green and Cole enough to seek a protective order against Skinner in early June of 2003. The order was never served; Cole and Green canceled it when Skinner promised to pay them off in MDMA pills. Hoping to distance themselves from Skinner, Cole and Green then turned to the DEA to inform them of Skinner's drug-related activities. Cole claimed Skinner had an MDMA lab at his mother's company in Tulsa. Green admitted to dealing for Skinner.

"I felt like Todd was going to kill her eventually," Green says. "And whether I loved her or not, my sole responsibility was to keep Krystle safe."

Green and Cole escaped to Las Vegas where they stayed in hotels and devised a plan to leave the country together. It was there, in the dry Nevada valley, that reality paid a rare visit.

"She [Krystle] realized that I'm a little boy of 18 and that I didn't have any finances, especially when there were no drugs to sell," Green recalls. "I wasn't going to be able to take care of her."

A few days into the Vegas trip, Cole asked Green to pick up some supplies from a health food store across town. When he returned, she was gone. She left a handwritten note for Green telling him that she had left for California to secure documents so the two of them could flee the country, and that he should return to Tulsa to await further contact[17]. Cole then returned to Tulsa, where she resumed her relationship with Skinner, who had plenty of cash and drugs[18]. Cole requested a protective order against Skinner on June 9, 2003; two weeks later, she showed up for an intimate, private gathering at Skinner's mother's house. With a small group of friends present, she planted herself next to Skinner and married him.

Confused, full of fear, and loathing the prospect of love lost, Green drove out of the Nevada desert and back to Oklahoma. He returned to the apartment he shared with Cole in Tulsa. After a few nights there, he came home and found Gordon Todd Skinner on his couch, uninvited.

---

17. In a 2006 cross-examination, Cole stated that she had gone to Oakland, California, at some point in her past and met with DEA agents. She was unable to recall when or how she got there. It may have been following the Nevada trip with Green.

18. Cole claims that she left Green because Skinner threatened to report her and Green to the DEA and that they would then face life imprisonment. Cole also claims that Skinner was aware that she and Green had spoken to the DEA by that point. According to Green, however, Cole called Skinner of her own volition, as they did not take cell phones with them to Las Vegas; this, of course, implies that Cole never really intended to escape Skinner. Skinner also claims that Cole called him and told him she wanted to get married. Green also recalls that the reason Cole told him she was going to California was to meet with members of the Brotherhood of Eternal Love to get false passports. Green claims he looked upon Cole as "his boss" and simply assumed she was in charge of their getaway.

"I couldn't believe it," Green says, "This was the very man I was hiding from and he was asleep in my living room."

What surprised Green even more, however, was that Skinner didn't seem upset with him. Skinner thanked Green for taking care of Cole. Skinner said he planned to leave the country with both of them to avoid governmental prosecution and offered up an idea for the three of them to begin a business venture that involved dredging harbors in the Caribbean. Green, still in love with Cole, felt unsure about the situation but agreed to the plans. Perhaps, he thought, he and Cole could ditch Skinner upon their arrival there. When he tried contacting Cole to discuss it with her, she wouldn't return his calls. Finally, Green met up with Skinner and Cole. Skinner handed him a document, a marriage certificate binding Cole and Skinner together. Skinner, Green claims, said that his marriage to Cole was just for legal reasons, and implied that it was fine with him if Green wanted to resume his relationship with Cole.[19]

"I didn't really know what to say and I just left," says Green. "And I was just numb. I went back to my roach-infested ghetto apartment and just sat there next to concrete, just up on some bricks, and just sat there."

For the next several days, Skinner, Cole, and Green did what drug users do. They continued to hang out and party.[20] Green remembers having sex with Cole while Skinner was showering. He didn't think Skinner would mind if he slept with his new bride, and Cole certainly didn't object.

ROOM 1411

From "Charges Allege Teen Kidnapped, Tortured," in the *Tulsa World*, reported on September 12, 2003:

---

19. Cole claims that when she returned from Vegas, Skinner dosed her and kept her drugged, and that he threatened her into marrying him—a story she has recounted in her book *MDMA for PTSD*. During her cross-examination, though, she did admit to being engaged to Skinner for a couple of years prior to the wedding though she said she was not planning to marry him.
20. Skinner believes that the reason Green was interested in hanging around was so that he could inform to the DEA about Skinner's activities. Green had recently been arrested on a drug charge in Lebanon, Missouri.

SUBTERRANEAN PSYCHONAUT

Three people were charged Thursday in a Tulsa County kidnapping in which the victim reportedly was held for six days and repeatedly tortured. Gordon Todd Skinner, Krystle Ann Cole Skinner and William Ernest Hauck were charged with kidnapping a Broken Arrow teenager during the Fourth of July weekend at the DoubleTree Hotel Downtown, 616 W. Seventh St. Police allege that the victim, 18, was held captive in the hotel, where he was tortured with beatings and chemical injections... The teen, broken, bloody and dehydrated, was found July 11 in a field in Texas City, Texas. Police picked him up and took him to a hospital.

From *Skinner vs. State of Oklahoma, June 11, 2009*:

Even a careful review of the record in this case leaves unanswered many questions about what exactly happened to 18-year-old Brandon Green, beginning over the Fourth of July weekend in 2003, at the hands of defendant Gordon Todd Skinner ("Skinner"), and with the assistance of his co-defendants Krystle Ann Cole Skinner ("Cole") and William Earnest Hauck ("Hauck"). It is even more unclear why it happened.

Originally, three people were charged in Green's kidnapping: Skinner, Cole, and Skinner's associate William Hauck. A fourth person, Kristi Roberts, never charged criminally, appears intermittently. Initially, they had all come together to celebrate the Fourth of July at the DoubleTree, some of them hoping to continue on to the Caribbean. Then, Brandon Green partook in a psychedelic rite, and everything went wrong. Each person's story is collected here, gathered from an assembly of interviews, public records, and private accounts. While no single story is endorsed, some light, however broken, reflects from their assembly.

KRISTI ROBERTS:
"EVERYTHING WILL BE ALL RIGHT"

"It's not as bad as it looks," Krystle Cole says to Kristi Roberts.

It's late at night on July 4 and Roberts pokes her head into Room 1411 of the DoubleTree Hotel in downtown Tulsa. Roberts had just met Cole and Skinner a few weeks ago, and they'd partied hard before, but not like this. Overturned food trays, fast-food containers, remnants of half-eaten meals, pillows, towels and linens are strewn across the room. There's dried vomit caked on the carpet. As she tiptoes toward the bathroom, she's bewildered by the site that unfolds.

Brandon Green, her "weed man," lies on the tile, his pants below his knees. Duct tape is strapped around his head and mouth, and his hands are taped behind his back and to his ankles. A KFC drink cup covers his genitals. Green had introduced her to Cole and Skinner, and now this? From behind her, Cole and Skinner explain that Green dropped way too much acid last night, Skinner estimates 15 sacramental wafers, and was out of control. They had to tie him up.

Roberts rummages around the room, finds a steak knife, and cuts Green free. He's not making much sense. Roberts has never seen anyone tripping as hard as he is. She draws a warm bath for him, and she sees Green's scrotum is so swollen it looks as though he has only one testicle. Green's not in the bath long before he defecates in the tub. Skinner steps forward and pulls Green out, and lifts him onto the bed. Skinner seems more agitated than usual. Roberts strokes Green's hair, telling him that everything will be all right.

With Skinner and Cole gone, Green calms down. He asks Roberts the same thing, a hundred times over: Does Krystle love me? Can you find out if she still loves me? Roberts promises to find out, but when Cole returns to the room she asks Roberts to go with her downstairs to ask the attendant something. When they get back up to the room, Green is passed out so deeply that he's drooling on the sheets. Skinner, she says, acts suspicious.

Subterranean Psychonaut

KRYSTLE COLE:
"HAUCK'S SCARING ME"

Paranoia and fear is all Cole seems to remember, according to her police statement. Hauck and Skinner, she claims, are both reporting to a federal agency, maybe the FBI or CIA.[21] She overhears them giving out their "agent numbers" on the telephone. She hears Hauck express repeated hopes to kill Green, but he never seems able to "get authorization." She believes there could be a team of nine other secret agents watching the hotel. She's not sure what to believe. What if Hauck is a cold-hearted contract killer?

"Hauck's scaring me. I mean this guy has no emotions," Cole says in court. "He time and time again said, 'This is too much trouble. Let's just kill Brandon and get it over with.' "

Skinner intervenes and insists that they should not kill Green, that he was only having a bad trip.

During some point at the DoubleTree, she doesn't say when, Cole sees Hauck pour a possibly potent drug, salvinorin C, into Green's mouth.[22] Cole rushes to Green's side when Hauck leaves the room. He sputters out some of the green stuff. A drop lands on Cole's arm, turning it entirely numb, she claims. Kristi Roberts shows up and together they put socks and plastic bags on their hands so they can untie and bathe Green without getting the potent chemical on their skin. The rash on Green's genitals is horrific from all the violent scratching. He has blood and tissue under his fingernails. Cole gets some ice and packs it onto Green's groin.

The night passes. Green's penis turns black near his ornamental piercing, the sign of a possible infection. Use antibiotics, she tells Skinner. Hauck and Skinner then shave off all the hair from Green's body. Skinner injects Green with vitamins and dextrose. Days later, Skinner examines

---

21. Hauck says that Skinner would ask him to pretend to be a secret agent in front of Cole, and he went along with the ruse without really understanding why.

22. Salvinorin is the psychotropic molecule in the natural hallucinogenic plant, *Salvia divinorum*. According to a 2001 report by the American Chemical Society, salvinorin C is reportedly inactive when taken by mouth. Court records suggest that Hauck was not present when Cole and/or Skinner gave Green the salvinorin.

Green again. He believes that gangrene has set in. They wash Green in a bath of Epsom salts, bleach, and chlorine. The fumes, Cole says, were so horrible that she was ill for two days.

BRANDON GREEN:
"I THOUGHT WE WERE FRIENDS"

After July 4, Green recalls very little, but he does have a vivid memory of waking up to the bursting pain of Skinner punting him in the groin.

"You should've never touched my fiancée," he hears Skinner shouting at him, and then everything goes white.

There's a moment of torture that repeatedly shows up in court records, and if it occurred, it would've been before Kristi Roberts showed up to bathe Green. Hauck claims he didn't see it, adding that Skinner only told him about it. A phone cord is wound around Green's genitals while he is unconscious. Skinner is allegedly at the other end of the line. He puts a foot down on Green's stomach, then pulls hard on the cord until the cartilage audibly snaps.

Later, as Green becomes more lucid and Roberts consoles him on the bed, Skinner walks into the room. Green apologizes to him for sleeping with Cole.

"I thought we were friends," Green says.

KRISTI ROBERTS:
"PLEASE PRAY FOR ME"

After caring for Green all night, Roberts eventually fell asleep at the DoubleTree. When she wakes up, Green is no longer there, and she believes Cole and Skinner when they tell her that Green left on his own. She helps clean up the room and discovers a couple of hypodermic needles in the bathroom and becomes even more suspicious of Cole and Skinner. Cole and Skinner decide to pack up and relocate to the Adam's Mark Hotel a few city blocks away, and Roberts rides with them. From the lobby of the Adam's Mark, Roberts calls her aunt and asks her to pray because she feels like she's trapped in a bad situation.

WILLIAM HAUCK:
"A FEAR OF TODD"

These days, Hauck drives a truck from 10 p.m. to 7 a.m. most nights, and he recently pulled over at a rest area to answer some questions about these decade-old events. He gives a plain, chronological account of the kidnapping and doesn't exaggerate when speaking. He shares Roberts' perception of Krystle Cole, saying she was clear-headed and lucid during the week-long ordeal. When asked if he saw Cole taking care of Green, Hauck's answer is flat.

"No," he says. "She wanted to go shopping. Todd had promised her they would go shopping."

She does go shopping, Hauck claims. Much later, after the rooms have been cleaned and Green has been relocated to Hauck's room, Hauck hears Cole offer a funny idea: Why don't they shave Green completely bald? Hauck watches as Skinner and Cole lather and shave Green's head. She applies eyeliner to the edges of Green's eyelids. Green is so gorked, he doesn't notice.

"Krystle thought it was hilarious," Hauck says. "She was shaving off his eyebrows and Todd told me that they had wanted to make him look gay… I was pretty freaked out," he says. "I knew that I was in pretty deep but there was nothing that I could do because at that point I had a fear of Todd. Todd started telling me how my involvement in everything would link back to my room and this was the only way out—to do it his way."

Skinner offers a plan to use Green's own car to dump him. Texas will find him, and they'll think he had a crazy weekend of partying. On the night of July 8, William Hauck drives the emaciated, drugged, and completely bald Brandon Green to a motel room in Texas City, Texas. Skinner says he and Cole will meet him tomorrow night.

THE DEA:
"HE SOUNDS A LITTLE SPOOKY"

The following day, July 9, Skinner is fed up with what he feels is a violation of his immunity agreements, marches into the DEA office in Tulsa with his attorney, H.I. Aston, and asks why the DEA is conducting an

MASON, SANDEL, AND CHAPMAN

investigation of him. In the next 24 hours, a flurry of emails ensues between DEA agents and government officials:

"Can you tell me what this guy [Skinner] was up to?" asks Tulsa Assistant US Attorney [AUSA] Allen Litchfield, a former classmate of Skinner, in an email. "He has popped into DEA claiming all types of immunity etc. Frankly he sounds a little spooky."

"Skinner was involved in an LSD deal," Lead AUSA Gregory Hough of Kansas replies. "His attorney got DOJ to give him immunity for his testimony against the other two leaders (Pickard and Apperson). After his testimony in the LSD trial, Skinner flipped back into the arms of his co-conspirators. This precipitated a bunch of mini-trials during our trial wherein Skinner, sponsored by Pickard and Apperson, testified that the three DEA agents, a courtroom deputy, and I all conspired to affect his trial testimony. Skinner alleged that, in spite of our best efforts, he testified truthfully. However, it was a tremendous distraction, likely caused OPR [Office of Professional Responsibility] investigations of all concerned and, at the least was a breach of his immunity agreement... I know three DEA agents, a courtroom deputy, and an AUSA that would love to see him imprisoned and the key thrown away."

BRANDON GREEN:
"HE JUST WANTS ME TO SLEEP"

When Skinner and Cole arrive at the motel in Texas City on the evening of July 9, Cole thinks that Green has a number of new needle tracks on his arms. Hauck had torn up the bed sheets and tied them around Green's wrists to keep him on the bed.[23] According to Hauck, Cole tells him and Skinner to do whatever they want to do, but she's going swimming in the hotel pool. In his confusion, Green continues to think that he and Cole are a couple. He feels ashamed for tripping so hard and apologizes repeatedly from within his stupor.

Skinner gives Green more injections, Hauck says. Skinner then brews a strange herbal concoction. After drinking it, Green feels a swell in his gut like he is about to explode. He vomits into the bathtub. Something

---

23. Hauck claims that Skinner gave him a syringe to use in the event Hauck needed to sedate Green, though he denies ever using it.

wiggles around in the mess. Cole says they look like worm sacks. Hauck sees tiny, translucent parasites writhing around in the bottom of the tub.

The next morning, July 10, Hauck and Cole search for a location where they can leave Green. If he's left outside, maybe the bug bites will cover all the needle marks. Hauck and Cole return and claim they've found an ideal spot to leave Green about a quarter of a mile away.

Inside the motel room, Green lies semi-conscious, with a blindfold over his eyes. Cole tells Green he burned his retinas and that he shouldn't try to open his eyes. Skinner then pretends he's a doctor from Sweden who has come to evaluate Green. Outside of Green's earshot, he explains that he wants Green to have a wholly unbelievable story. The Swedish doctor will make Green a less reliable historian.

When evening arrives, Hauck loads Green into the car and Cole follows him in Skinner's Porsche. Skinner stays at the hotel and waits.

"I remember feeling safe with [Hauck]. I remember feeling at peace," Green said of the car ride to the field. "He put his arm over me, and just patted me and said, 'Just stay there,' and I fell back asleep."

En route to the field, Hauck stops at a convenience store and tells Cole to buy water and food for Green. She returns with two bottles of water and some Kit Kat Bites. When they reach the open field, Hauck drives Green's car off the road about a hundred feet from the roadway and stops. He sets a blanket down on the ground near the car, and then opens the car door to get Green.

"William comes by, unbuckles me, grabs me like a baby and puts me on the grass," Green said. "I remember thinking, 'William is so nice. He knows how tired I am. He just wants me to sleep.' The earth felt really nice. The earth felt really, really, nice, and I just fell asleep."

Hauck sets the Kit Kat Bites and two bottles next to Green, then climbs into the car Cole is driving. The car pulls away, leaving Brandon Green alone under the Texas night sky, little more than flesh for flies.

GORDON TODD SKINNER:
"NO ONE IS GOOD OR BAD"

According to Skinner, there hasn't been a fair trial for the Green kidnapping. During the research period for this story, Skinner was able to briefly review a copy of Cole's book, *Lysergic*, which contains a number of letters that Skinner allegedly sent to Cole during his incarceration.[24]

"I went to the DEA and got you out of trouble," Skinner reportedly wrote, "you brought Brandon into my life and I got hurt bad. I asked both of you to leave for good—do you remember that??? Not only did I not lure him back to the hotel—I begged you to get him out of my room/life... The two of you should've stayed away from me." The letter goes on to explain how Green and Cole "were sexual" in the hotel bed the first night at the DoubleTree while Skinner slept next to them. "That was wrong, I told both of you," the letter states. Today, in his drab prison blues, Skinner carries all the intimidation of your average high school science teacher.

"There was no way anyone could've come out alright," Skinner says. "The only way that anyone could've come out decent was if the truth was told, which was that this guy [Green] purely overdosed himself... No one is good or bad. It's not like it's that kind of story."

In Skinner's estimation of events, the entire week was more sedate than other witnesses recollected. His young children from an earlier marriage visited the hotel room, he says.

Skinner says that the entire Green kidnapping was an elaborate government conspiracy and cites the emails between Hough and Litchfield as evidence. He also contends he was far too ill during most of the Green incident to be as involved as the others allege.

"I had been to the hospital numerous times..." he says. "I was really sick—I just couldn't coagulate blood. Every hotel room I had, had blood in it." Green saw Skinner's nosebleeds, and even admitted taking Skinner to the hospital four times in four consecutive days the week prior to the kidnapping.

Green believes he saw Skinner kick him and yell at him, yet Skinner denies it.

"He also says the most incredible things [in his testimonies]," Skinner says. "But what was going on with him? He was on a massive dose of psychedelics."

Green's trauma must've been self-induced, Skinner thinks. He says that Hauck is the one who tied Green up, and that he helped Roberts

---

24. Skinner believes the letters may have been augmented, but he has not been able to fully review the book.

SUBTERRANEAN PSYCHONAUT

free Green. Hauck does admit to tying Green up, but only in Texas, and Hauck admits to hitting Green as well. Skinner points to Green's infected penis piercing and his incessant genital scratching as evidence of the self-harm. Moreover, Green was left alone with Hauck for long periods, and Hauck had served time for a sex-related offense, suggesting that the extensive anal damage could've been done then.

"I don't like talking about all this stuff," says Skinner. "I don't come from a trashy world, OK? But I'm having to defend myself and everything... This guy [Green] was hell on wheels, for days he was like this."

AFTERMATH

Pain is Brandon Green's constant companion now. It took him months to get out of his wheelchair, a year to begin eating solid foods. Now, 10 years after his kidnapping, his body is riddled with ongoing pain. On a scale of 1–10, with 10 being the most severe pain, Green ranks his neck a 4–6. His shoulders are a 5 on a good day (he still can't lay on his left side). His hips, pelvis, prostate, and groin hurt so badly that it's painful to wear pants. Green doesn't carry a cell phone or wallet because their pressure against his body hurts too much. Bad days are 8s.

"I honestly do not remember at all life without pain; I cannot remember a day I didn't hurt," says Green, who abstains from the dulling effects of pain medication.

Work, for Green, is a refuge. He and his wife manage a condominium complex together. Someday, Green would like to begin telling his story publicly. After some of his health returned, in the first few years following the kidnapping, Green returned to a number of illegal activities involving drugs and pimping. He has since disavowed those ways. He's now a religious man and believes his Christianity has helped him transcend much of the anger, depression, fear, and confusion that could otherwise plague his mind. But forgiveness, for Green, doesn't mean forgetting.

"I think that Todd is pretty pissed that he did not kill me," says Green. "You know, knowing Todd, I bet his biggest regret is that he didn't snap my neck a month prior to the kidnapping. I would love to hug the guy, but I would be afraid he would kill me."

During the legal proceedings following the kidnapping, the Assistant Tulsa District Attorney David Robertson told Brandon Green that the charges against Krystle Cole would be changed. Cole, Robertson explained, was simply a wayward small-town girl. He parroted the same alibi that Green recalled Cole practicing in the Las Vegas hotel room. Green felt nauseated. The courts amended Cole's charge to "accessory after the fact." She pleaded no contest. On March 26, 2007, she was ordered to pay a restitution of $52,109. According to Green, she paid little more than $4,000 and was released from the order.

"I could have fought the case and won," Cole wrote in *Lysergic*. "Since I was under duress and basically kidnapped also."

Bette Brown, the case manager who filed Cole's 2007 "Finding of Fact – Acceptance of Plea," pointed out that Cole stayed with Skinner for years, and "does not appear to be someone who is afraid of their spouse." Brown believed that Cole participated in Green's kidnapping more than she admitted. Brown recommended incarceration. Cole's sentence was deferred. Her probation for her role in the kidnapping lasted five years. She served no time.

Cole is now a self-made entheogen expert, just as Skinner had been, but Cole is much more popular. She has created dozens of videos about "responsible drug use." Her YouTube channel boasts 54,167 subscribers, and at least 10 of her videos have been viewed a quarter-million times each. Throughout her videos and her writings, Cole claims she suffers from post-traumatic stress disorder. She told the court in 2007 that she had no mental health issues.

Cole often presents herself as a survivor, one who has experienced a terrible life event and has moved to a more spiritual understanding of herself and her relationship to Skinner. But, in a 2009 post on her website, Cole claimed she's tormented by nightmares when she's reminded of Skinner. Cole also said she had not granted permission to use her name, likeness, book, or life story when we contacted her with questions for this article. Green, seeking closure and understanding, attempted to contact Cole several times in recent years, to no avail; she replied to Green's messages soon after hearing from us. She convinced him, for a short time, that she tried to rescue him during the kidnapping. "Honestly, I believe you," Green wrote in an email to Cole. Cole then asked Green for his permission to publish their email exchange (with her edits) on her website. Then Green heard Hauck's version of the events. He felt once again betrayed by Cole.

"How could I be so gullible?" he asked.

If Green senses that justice has not been served, it's in the matter of Krystle Cole's involvement.

"Krystle should be in jail," he says. "I feel like Todd is on the last end of his crazy life, but Krystle is at the very beginning of it. Krystle has been trained by the very best. I would feel more comfortable with Todd being out of jail than Krystle staying free…. I feel like Todd's ceiling is Krystle's floor. That is why I feel like she is more dangerous. I feel like she was able to consume everything Todd had, then pushed him out of the way and continued going."[25]

For his willingness to testify against Skinner, William Hauck's charges were amended to "accessory after the fact." Hauck is a barrel-shaped man, with gray hair and a goatee. Since testifying against Skinner, he claims there's been two attempts on his life. He found bullet holes in the side of his truck one morning; on another, a gas can was wired to his car. On Sunday, June 16, 2013, Green and Hauck reunited. It was the first time either of them had spoken or seen each other since the trial. Hauck was apprehensive at first. Upon arrival, Green hugged Hauck without a word.

"If I were you," he told Green, "I would've brought a big gun to this meeting."

Green told Hauck that he's forgiven him and moved on with his life.

"For a long time, even after the trial, I couldn't sleep," Hauck said. "I couldn't look at myself in the mirror. I wasn't only embarrassed, I was ashamed."

"Why didn't they actually kill me?" Green asked him. "Because it would have been better for them to just kill me."

"At that time, I was involved in it, and that wasn't going to happen," Hauck said. "I mean, dumping you off in the woods and letting you find your own way out was one thing, but killing you was—I would have picked up the phone at that point."

Hauck answered all of Green's remaining questions for over two hours, filling in gaps and questions that Green carried, many of them having to do with Krystle's behavior during the kidnapping. At the end

---

25. In 2011, Cole acted as the primary government witness against one of the advertisers on her website, Clark Sloan, an individual who was allegedly selling illegal substances. He was indicted with twenty drug-related counts.

of the questioning, Green told Hauck that he hoped he might find the strength to forgive himself.

"Even if I were able to forgive myself," Hauck replied, "I would never be able to *really* forgive myself."

William Leonard Pickard is appealing his case while serving life imprisonment in Tucson, Arizona. He contends that he was the victim of a con orchestrated by Skinner. In 2005, Cole filed an affidavit with the U.S. Court of Appeals stating that Skinner owned the Wamego lab equipment, Skinner was in fact the chemist, and Skinner told her that he planned to setup Pickard up as the responsible party in the LSD operation.

"This is what you do when you get hot," Cole says she heard Skinner say, "you turn the other people in before you get busted."

Pickard is now 67 years old. Outside of his legal filings, he primarily reads literature published between the years 1840 and 1920. He actively updates the site freeleonardpickard.org and uses student volunteers to facilitate his email communication.

During their respective appeals process, Skinner's and Pickard's attorneys have maintained occasional communication. Pickard claims to have met Cole on only one occasion, and has not read her book. Cole's actions have done little to help his situation.

"She is also deleterious to the case by promoting her various fantasies, derived largely from her brief marriage to an unreliable informant, or from her scrutiny of documents concerning sophisticated interactions about which she has little experience in interpreting," Pickard wrote from prison. "Some feel she frantically is scrambling to some peak of notoriety in the absence of other distinguishing accomplishments. We, as observers, are saddened...The spectacle of Cole commenting on the case to her profit, eagerly filling a void that has not yet been addressed by the principals, is rather as if Judas's wife was the sole public source of information on the Crucifixion."

In an odd turn of events, Pickard has recently been calling Brandon Green, with the explanation that he would simply like to be friends. Green enjoys the calls, he says.

In June of 2006, a jury found Gordon Todd Skinner guilty of kidnapping, assault, and conspiracy of kidnapping. The jury sentenced

SUBTERRANEAN PSYCHONAUT

Skinner to life for the assault charge, and 90 years for kidnapping and conspiracy; Skinner was already incarcerated at that point for drug-related crimes concerning activities at a Burning Man festival. Skinner claims that his immunity agreements were violated when the DEA cooperated with the Tulsa Police Department's kidnapping investigation of Skinner.

"Who cares about the DEA hating you?" he asks. "That's like a badge of honor if those guys hate you because it means you must have done something right."

From the letters in the back of *Lysergic*, it appears that Skinner has formed new spiritual understandings while incarcerated. One letter states:

> The Brotherhood of Eternal Love and its ilk were another spiritual con game. These people in the Network were there for the money—I used to say gift everything to prove your point. LSD Network was a high class drug Network—but money (MAMMON) oriented—Not Spiritual—but do not teach each one how to be their own Priest? Just a power game…Do you think I have gained wealth, fame or power from this road? I bow and pray each day and remember the True Sacrament of life is LOVE.

Skinner is still technically married to Krystle Cole—for legal reasons, he says. He plans to sign the divorce papers soon. He claims he doesn't feel betrayed by Cole, not exactly.

"I mean, it wasn't betrayal," Skinner said. "She was involved in a massive conspiracy that went on for years and she admits to it."

He's not the kind of guy who has regrets, he says, but he clearly feels the pain of imprisonment. He continues to file appeals outlining the various injustices he claims he's suffered at the hands of the DEA and government officials. Should the appeals be unsuccessful, Skinner's earliest hope for parole would be when he's about 80 years old.

"I've spent ten years of my life—my life's been threatened, I've been greatly harmed, I have lost everything, and the paper trail is overwhelming of what has been done to me," he says.

149

MASON, SANDEL, AND CHAPMAN

The trail of what Skinner has done to others is stacked just as high. Both of those trails converge behind the gray walls of Joseph Harp Correctional Center, Skinner's home. Unless a new trail appears, Gordon Todd Skinner remains trapped in the worst trip he has ever taken.

WEIRD AL-CHEMY

Tracing Weird Al Yankovic's steps through Tulsa during the filming of the cult classic 'UHF'

BY *Mitch Gilliam*

"YOU DON'T KNOW WHAT LIFE BEFORE AL WAS LIKE," said my longtime co-worker Kevin "Okie" Okey. He's delivered pizza from the downtown Tulsa Mazzio's since it was a Pizzettis, "since *Alapalooza* and before *Bad Hair Day*," he said. That's 20 years, for the uninitiated.

Okey is right; I can't imagine life before Weird Al. For me—and many others—Al is, has, and always will be around. He's the guy with the goofy versions of pop songs. He's the guy with the hair and the accordion. Weird Al Yankovic is as American as Cheez Whiz on a hot dog in a Twinkie. I don't know how life before Al felt, but Okey remembers accepting him into his. "I saw the video for 'Eat It' first," he recalls. "Nickelodeon was airing *Turkey TV* at the time, and I remember seeing more of his videos on there. When 'Dare To Be Stupid' came out, I thought, wow, I need to get into this guy." There may be crazier fans, but Okey was my hierophant to the world of Al.

Before I met Okey I didn't know there are people who listen to comedy rock 90 percent of the time. He may be among the less fervent, but his overall existence is Yankovician in itself. He has heterochromatic eyes, practices Fushigi, and married a woman with the same first and middle name as his sister. He's a homunculus of the Weird Alchemist, a thought-form made flesh through pure wacky willpower. "There

MITCH GILLIAM

will be two Elizabeth Anne Okeys at Weird Al's anniversary show," he proudly told me.

UHF, Weird Al's only feature film, was shot in Tulsa in 1988. It's a goofball movie with characters as odd and endearing as Okey. A love letter to public access television and social outcasts, it follows a barely there "band together and save our ship" narrative over a UHF station, U-62. Co-written by Al and manager/director Jay Levey, it bombed at the box office, but became a cult hit. More acclaimed films may have been shot in Tulsa, but none of them have *UHF*'s ring of Dadaist documentary edge. Kevin Okeys are still buying whoopee cushions and writing Klingon versions of "Who's on First."

Specters from the shoot permeate Tulsa. Poodles fly from an apartment by Okey's Mazzio's. Al flies from Billy Ray's BBQ on east 15th street. Karate students fly from the windows above Downtown Lounge. From U-62's antenna near Sand Springs to Ernie Miller Pontiac by 41st and Memorial, nearly all of Tulsa is humorously haunted. Even mundane locations seem important to Al. He rattles off every address on the DVD commentary, allowing the less astute to make the *UHF* pilgrimage of the pious. Tulsans pick out locations when they watch the film, but some realize they're watching them from the inside.

We were watching *UHF* at the 401 Club when we realized the room we were sitting in was Al's apartment," said Jeff Pierce, the defunct punk venue's owner.

But why Tulsa? The answer to that is innocuous enough: convenience. Tulsa's half-vacant Kensington Galleria was a mall/hotel that the crew could film and sleep in. Executive Producer Gray Frederickson acknowledged the facility's importance to me. But then there was the *niceness*.

"I have a story I tell folks in Hollywood," Frederickson told me. On *The Outsiders*, which he also produced, Frederickson had a run-in with the Teamsters Union. Francis Ford Coppola had cut half of their trucks from the production, and the head of the Tulsa Teamsters at the time, Coleman Davis, confronted Frederickson. "He was gonna fight. He pulled out his front teeth and put them in his pocket," remembered Frederickson. They came to an agreement, but Frederickson avoided the union altogether when he returned to Tulsa for *UHF*. The first day of filming was sweltering, and had the crew working outdoors. Frederickson spied Davis approach, and the union boss let him know he was standing

154

WEIRD AL-CHEMY

in front of the Teamsters' hall. Frederickson thought Davis would pull out his teeth again, but Davis invited the crew out of the heat instead. The non-union group ate lunch in unionized air conditioning, and Davis was given a part in the film.

Frederickson, who also produced *Rumblefish*, describes Tulsa as "your own giant back lot." The extras are plentiful, and fire fighters are happy to turn a dry street into a rainy set. That affability was something he advertised, but he, Yankovic, and Levey were surprised by the oddity they found in residence. The script called for a telethon scene of odd talents, so a casting call was staged, pulling Okeys out of thin air. "We had guys coming in standing on their heads playing banjos, singing out of their stomachs," said Frederickson. Charles Marsh, who passed away last July, made it to television with his upside-down yodeling. The Uncle Sam on stilts and grotesque dancing stomachs were also found on location. Of all the telethon acts, only West Coast weirdos The Kipper Kids had to be flown in.

With a cast full of faces that went on to be familiar, nearly every other actor is an Okie. Lisa Stefanic, as "Wheel of Fish" contestant Phyllis Weaver, offers the best acting in the movie that isn't slapstick. Her image made it onto posters for *UHF*, and her jubilation turned to pain at the gain and loss of a red snapper is a scene that resonates with viewers internationally. Local comic Barry Friedman tried out for a French waiter part, only to be cast as one of the main villain's "yes men" along with a Kevin Roden in a cowboy hat and fake mustache. Former RSU professor Eldon Hallum was the "Spatula City Dad," giving the character a perfect slack-jawed forehead slap. Everyone in the "Spatula City" scene was local, and every extra in every scene was, too. Friedman noted the film's gracious credits, quipping, "Al gave a title to every person he saw while driving around town. *Apocalypse Now* has a shorter cast list." The locals still reap the benefits of their roles. Friedman boasts about the $3.76 he gets when the film plays in Lithuania. Stefanic remembers standing behind someone renting *UHF* at Blockbuster and having one of her kids whisper, "Mom, we can afford pizza tonight."

Almost all the Tulsans in the film came from The Linda Layman Agency. Don Hull, Layman's husband and booking agent, invited me to his office to talk about the movie. He had a photo of Al, Victoria Jackson, and himself ready for me. Hull told me he was an extra in a scene with

Jackson and kept the photo as a souvenir. While I eyed the photograph Don handed me another. It was a large signed photo of Al with all of the extras in the "Spatula City" scene. In it, Al sits above the crowd, arms extended, victorious. He signed it with his name and "Thank you Spatula City Shoppers!" On Don's desk was a coffee mug, laminated with a picture of Al and "Little Old Lady" Wilma Jeanne Cummins, who passed away in 2011. She, like Charles Marsh, made it to TV with her odd talent. Playing pop bottles as musical instruments, her act went unused in the film, perhaps a testament to the wealth of weird the crew dug up. *UHF* memorabilia dominated Hull's workspace—a lonely photo of Chuck Norris was the only thematically irrelevant artifact.

If Okey is Yankovic's Golem, the overall production is his hyper-sigil. With Al as a sorcerer, *UHF* is his condensation of will into celluloid, where the on-screen action bleeds through and pierces the corporeal. Much how Al and team found weirdness where it lay through hopeful casting, the production of the film mirrored U-62's push for group ownership and the power of the bizarre. Hull recalled the guerrilla nature of the production: drilling fish onto spinning wheels, posting flyers for K.C.-lit trucks at off-roading clubs, and his scene, where Joey's House of Blues doubles as a dive bar and the four-star restaurant at which he pretends to dine. Even the "Spatula City" billboard loomed over Highway 51 for a full summer. The final scene of the movie, a huge crowd endeavor to purchase the studio from the villains, was filmed over several nights in a field. Michael Richards, playing the blueprint for *Seinfeld*'s Cosmo Kramer, had to keep the crowd awake and screaming until dawn. His real life actions took on the role of his character, telling the locals any good takes would get them into his hotel for "chocolate pudding and cheese." Hull said that two weeks of *UHF* was "like going to LA for a year." Locations and people weren't the limit of Tulsa's imprint on the project. Stunts were coordinated by Tulsa bomb technician Robert Maras, who played a thug and donated his son to the famous "fire hose" scene. The trains for Stanley Spadowki's Clubhouse were built by the Green Country Model Railroaders Association, and Al's car in the film, a Nash Metropolitan, was procured from a Tulsa owner. Richards sought out the local Shriners for his mini car. The owner at the time, Ken Deatherage, remembers Yankovic, Richards, and Jackson arriving in a limo to view it. "I gave them all tomatoes from my garden, and it

WEIRD AL-CHEMY

blew their minds," he told me, "because they were all born on concrete and had never tasted a real one."

Just as the filming paralleled the script, so does the community narrative surrounding it. When local station RSU-TV needed help with funding they reached out to Yankovic. He returned their call. A telethon was staged in early October with local *UHF* stars, and Al appeared at several functions for their benefit. Last month Circle Cinema played Al's failure of a film to 500 people on three sold-out screens. Yankovic, Levey, and Frederickson sat in for a Q&A. Film posters by locals and Twinkie wiener sandwiches, the film's snack legacy, were sold as concessions.

Fans can, and do, heed Al's call. They visit locations from the film and find a city just as odd as the one they've idolized on screen. The *Chainsaw Massacre* house is now a train-themed restaurant, but Tulsa is just the same—a Petrie dish teeming with Okey-like microbes. When Okey's Beetle broke down, he got a smaller Fiat for his 20-plus pizza catering jobs. That's dedication to form from a man who truly "dares to be stupid." I told Okey I'd be interviewing Al, in case he had a burning question he needed answered. Without hesitation he replied: "Will he sign my adoption papers?"

POP LIFE

An artist from Idabel recalls his cosmopolitan adventures

By *Steve Sherman*

HAROLD STEVENSON IS A TINY 84-YEAR-OLD MAN wearing a knit shirt with a frayed collar. He lives in a log cabin nestled in a small pine forest outside of Idabel, Oklahoma, his hometown. Idabel is far into southeastern Oklahoma—if you were to roll a basketball from the top of the hill by Harold's cabin, it would stop near Texas. Harold's porch has rotten boards covered by rugs, and his shepherd mixes are fond of licking my ears. Behind his cabin is a huge storage room/studio stacked with the dusty detritus of his glamorous life: half-finished paintings of nude men, frescoed rococo furniture, and photo albums from his Hamptons years.

Harold has been an artist since he was four years old and has never thought about being anything else. He once mounted a four-story painting onto the Eiffel Tower. His most famous work is called *The New Adam;* it is an 8-feet-tall by 40-feet-long male nude. At the center of that painting is an uncircumcised penis—"in the Guggenheim, a Jewish museum!"

When living in Athens, Paris, London, New York City, and Venice, Harold always carried Idabel with him. Ask him about his close friend Andy Warhol, for whom Harold helped coordinate his first gallery exhibit in New York City, and Harold will quickly divert to anecdotes about Helen Rose, the girl who lived across the street from his boyhood home. Ask him what his parents thought about Igor Stravinsky, Anthony Perkins,

STEVE SHERMAN

or any of the other luminaries whom Harold brought to Idabel over the years; ask him, and he will tell you that his parents didn't think much of them. Then he will go back to waxing about Helen Rose. Despite living everywhere and "meeting everyone of importance in the world," Harold claims he "never left Idabel."

"I was the most celebrated person to arrive in Idabel, and I arrived by birth, on March 11, 1929, in a brick bungalow on Avenue A," Harold says as we sit on his porch. He says by age four he was already an artist. By age 10, he claims to have been un-teachable by local art instructors. So Harold acquired studio space in a three-story building downtown.

"I painted all the people who came there, and that was everybody," he says.

Mitchell Algus, Harold's gallery representative since 1992, recalls asking Harold if he was teased for being gay in school. Harold replied, "Honey, I owned that school."

"I was a local phenomenon," Harold tells me.

At age 17 Harold began attending the University of Oklahoma, where he met the man who would become his longtime lover, a Choctaw named Lloyd Tugwell. At the urging of architect Bruce Goff, Harold moved to New York City in 1949. On his first day there, Harold seduced a "startlingly beautiful" male ballet dancer. Later, Harold met Alexander Iolas, the Hugo Gallery's proprietor, and soon earned patronage and gallery support. With Iolas' help, Harold set up a show for his new friend, a Ruthenian American from Pittsburgh named Andy Warhol. Iolas also connected Harold to major surrealist painters of the era: Pavel Tchelitchew, Max Ernst, and others.

Harold spent most of the 1950s in New York City, and then moved to Paris towards the end of the decade; gallerist Iris Clert was Harold's major supporter there. Harold painted his most famous works in Paris. These include *Eye of Lightning Billy*, a colossal painting of a hand with an eye in the palm. This painting was included in the *International Exhibition of the New Realists* at the Sidney Janis Gallery in 1962, considered *the* landmark exhibit in Pop Art's popular emergence. Harold's work was displayed alongside pieces by Warhol, Roy Lichtenstein, and Robert Indiana.

Next was *The New Adam*, the aforementioned monumental nude in the Guggenheim. The uncircumcised model for the painting was the

160

POP LIFE

actor Sal Mineo, best known for his role in *Rebel Without a Cause* ("He was a sweetheart person, and kind of stupid," Harold says).

Then there was *El Cordobes*, a four-story portrait of the famous Spanish bullfighter that was affixed to the Eiffel Tower in 1963. There are pictures of Harold smoking a cigarette in front of the installation, standing next to Ms. Clert and designer Yves Saint-Laurent. Harold, handsome with a sideways part, looks as if he's in the middle of telling everyone a joke.

———————

After Harold finishes his catfish at David Beard's, we take a driving tour of Idabel.

"There wasn't anything here," Harold says as we drive down Washington Street, past Denison Cemetery (where Lloyd is buried), past newer subdivisions, and a Braum's. Harold is fond of the breakfast at Braum's, he says. He shows us his old brick bungalow and Helen Rose's old stone house.

I turn onto Central Avenue and drive past a strip of empty Plains Commercial buildings.

Downtown Idabel has almost disappeared, he says, including the beautiful red brick courthouse. I turn through wide downtown streets; I don't see anyone walking around. I park in front of his old studio building, in which he was on the second story. He can't remember who occupied the ground floor. Next door is a shop that will buy your gold.

"There's nothing much more to it," Harold says as we drive away from downtown Idabel, down the two-lane highway and back to the torrid cabin and the dogs.

I have seen pictures from last decade of Harold and Lloyd in their former home in the Hamptons: Inside are four-foot-tall ferns, cement palm tree finials on top of decorative columns, tiger print throw pillows.

Lloyd died last decade. Harold cannot recall details about what Lloyd cooked, and he sometimes pauses at length between sentences. Behind Harold's sweltering cabin is an unfinished studio/storage with exposed insulation wrapping. Inside that space his old animal print furniture is stacked and covered with white dust, and those old decorative columns are piled on the walls and blocked by half-painted studies of nude men. I imagine that opportunists could raid his collection of valuables. A

STEVE SHERMAN

gentleman at the Main Street Café later confirmed these fears. Another friend accused local scammers of taking Harold's art and placing it on eBay.

Harold continued to paint in the 1970s and '80s and lived in the Dakota in Central Park West. He gallivanted around Venice with Warhol and Peggy Guggenheim, and bought residences in Long Island City and Key West, all while Lloyd cooked ("Lloyd loved meat"), decorated the home, and drove Harold around in his big Cadillac.

By 1990, Clert and Iolas were dead, and Harold's notoriety (at least in the United States) had waned. According to Algus, in the more conservative art world of the 1960s, '70s, and '80s, Harold's blatantly homoerotic paintings cost him showings. For example, *The New Adam* was refused for the Guggenheim's landmark *Six Painters and the Object* exhibit on the grounds that its monumental nudity would distract "the whole weight of public attention" to the painting.

Though the Guggenheim now, ironically, keeps *The New Adam*, the painting hasn't been on display there since 2006. Harold's other major works, like the *Eye of Lightning Billy,* are currently in a private collection, as is *Raft of Medusa.*

That last painting currently resides in Idabel, though at one point in time it was supposed to be in the Whitney Museum of American Art in New York, according to Mitchell Algus. Through Harold, Algus had coordinated a donation of the painting to the Whitney. According to Algus, the truck driver for the shipping company arrived to take the painting to New York, but was met by Harold's (now former) nephew-in-law holding a gun. That person refused to answer my inquiries. Harold's nephew, Kurt, who was present the day of the failed delivery, was not able to get a definitive answer from the Whitney about the donation. He thought it was another attempt to scam Harold, as there had been many at that time. The Whitney, likewise, never responded to my inquiries. Algus produced receipts from Artemis Fine Art Services of Dallas, Texas, showing the cost of transit for taking *Raft of Medusa* from Idabel to the Whitney. Regardless, that painting is not in the Whitney as of today.

In 2005 Lloyd died; he fell down the stairs at their Hamptons home. Harold's family buried him in the family plot in Idabel.

POP LIFE

Soon Harold sold the Hamptons home and moved back to the cabin in the woods.

"I still haven't quite recovered from [Lloyd's death]," Harold says in rare moment of modesty. His nieces and nephew help him around the house, and "even going to the grocery store is difficult."

Harold's life now entails dinner parties, the occasional Grey Goose martini, and deliberately occupying the idea of his boyhood Idabel. Despite the books one could write retracing his career and friendships and paintings, Pop Art luminary and painter of monuments Harold Stevenson seems aware of his station in life.

"You see," he says, "I've always been the most famous artist in Idabel, Oklahoma."

BORROWED NOTES

Sanora Babb and John Steinbeck in the race for the great
American Dust Bowl novel

By *Cortney Stone*

In 1939, John Steinbeck's *The Grapes of Wrath* became a best-seller and turned the nation's attention to the plight of migrant farmers escaping the Dust Bowl. The novel's central characters represented Oklahoma in public memory, giving the state a reputation as a place of tragedy and poverty. Many Oklahomans condemned the novel as an obscene misrepresentation.

Ask red-dirt-blooded Oklahomans today about *The Grapes of Wrath*, and you'll probably receive a disgusted look—either because they do not want to be in the same category as the low-class Joads or because the book bored them to death in high school. Unfortunately, many do not know that while Steinbeck's Dust Bowl novel was revealing a public crisis and embarrassing Oklahomans, a Dust Bowl novel from an Oklahoman was silenced.

CORTNEY STONE

Born in Oklahoma in 1907, Sanora Babb grew up in the hard life of busted-out farms in the Oklahoma Panhandle, Colorado, and Kansas. As a girl, Babb decided that she would write about the farmers of the arid High Plains—her people. In 1929, she moved to Los Angeles to further her career. Her social life grew to include artists such as Ralph Ellison—with whom she had a love affair—and Chinese-American cinematographer James Wong Howe. She married Howe, violating California's anti-miscegenation laws, and she became involved with progressive causes and the Communist Party.

In 1938, Babb worked for the Farm Security Administration as the assistant to Tom Collins, the manager of FSA camps in California. The camps provided support for refugees displaced by drought, dust storms, and the loss of their farms. Babb lived in the camps and provided refugees with medical attention and education about sanitation and workers' rights. She saw them exploited by growers, despised by locals, and turned away from hospitals and stores. She watched refugees suffer from starvation and illness through the winter months when there was no work. She supported striking workers and went to jail. She respected the refugees as good people who wanted work, not charity. Because she was from Oklahoma, the refugees trusted Babb and shared their stories with her, so Collins had her take field notes and write FSA reports. Babb also began planning a novel that would show how much her people were suffering.

She was not the only person with that idea. John Steinbeck had already written two Dust Bowl novels and was developing another about migrant farmers. He visited the camps for several weeks in 1936 and helped rescue refugees from floods for 10 days during the winter of 1937–38. Eventually, Collins gave him copies of Babb's notes to use for his novel, and Steinbeck hurried home to write. Babb remained in the camps until October 1938 and by the time she began writing her own novel, Steinbeck had written most of *The Grapes of Wrath*.

In 1939, Babb sent excerpts of her novel *Whose Names Are Unknown* to Random House, and the publisher was eager to print it. When *The Grapes of Wrath* came out later that year, Random House decided they could not follow such a huge success with a similar publication. Babb stashed the manuscript in a drawer and quietly continued her career. Meanwhile, *The Grapes of Wrath* won a Pulitzer Prize and became a motion picture, and Steinbeck reigned as the champion of the people.

BORROWED NOTES

The rejection seems to be a mere misfortune, but examining *Whose Names Are Unknown* and *The Grapes of Wrath* side by side shows it is an injustice against Babb, Oklahoma, and the refugees. Both authors used the same notes and had been in the camps, but Babb had far more firsthand experience than Steinbeck. Though Steinbeck's work is sympathetic and based on truth, the novel still has grave inaccuracies and shortcomings. Babb's novel, however, is thoroughly detailed and accurate, and she shows greater respect toward the refugees.

Both novels begin in Oklahoma with farming families. Steinbeck's Joads live near Sallisaw, and while his descriptions of the Dust Bowl are accurate, they could not have applied to eastern Oklahoma, which was nowhere near the Dust Bowl. Babb begins her novel with the Dunne family in the Oklahoma Panhandle—the only part of the state with severe Dust Bowl damage—and her descriptions of the environment are vivid and realistic. Steinbeck knew Oklahoma through photographs and a highway map, but Babb had lived in Oklahoma and breathed its air.

Both families lose their farms to the banks and decide to move to California in search of work, but the authors approach this differently. Steinbeck tells the story through dramatic dialogue and artistic meanderings on preparing, packing, and traveling on Route 66. His Okies speak in heavy dialect and use poor grammar, and their offenses include drinking, swearing, making obscene comments, sexual immorality, and violence. In contrast, Babb focuses on the Dunnes' life in Oklahoma, establishing what the family has and who they are, before skipping straight to their resettlement in California to show what they have lost and who they have become. The Dunnes and their neighbors use very little dialect, and Babb portrays them as moral people with normal human flaws. The Joads seem like flat characters crafted for a story, while the Dunnes appear to be a respectful amalgamation of people Babb knew personally in the FSA camps.

Though both writers describe the harsh conditions in California, Babb goes further than Steinbeck with the story. She shows deep sympathy and intimacy as she elaborates on working conditions, labor strikes, the hard winter, and the extreme near-starvation the families experienced. Steinbeck includes these issues, but not to the same extent.

Whose Names Are Unknown and *The Grapes of Wrath* are both great American Dust Bowl novels that emerged at the same time

CORTNEY STONE

with different perspectives. Steinbeck hit shelves in 1939; Babb waited until 2004, when University of Oklahoma Press published *Whose Names* the year before her death. Babb tells a realistic story about credible characters in straightforward language, but Steinbeck is an outsider crafting a tale in pseudo-biblical language and scraggly dialect. In the end, Steinbeck's work won the publishing race, but Babb's work remains a voice that cannot be manipulated or silenced.

SEARCHING FOR JOHN JOSEPH MATHEWS

On the trail of one of the Osage Nation's most important writers

By *Richard Higgs*

He showed his anger in fantastic play of lightning, and thunder that crashed and rolled among the hills; in the wind that came from the great tumbling clouds which appeared in the northwest and brought twilight and ominous milk-warm silence. His beneficence showed on April mornings when the call of the prairie chicken came rolling over the awakened prairie and the killdeer seemed to be fussing; on June days when the emerald grass sparkled in the dew and soft breezes whispered, the quail whistled and the autumnal silences when the blackjacks were painted like dancers and dreamed in the iced sunshine with fatalistic patience.

—*Sundown* by John Joseph Mathews, 1934

"I THINK I HEAR ONE!" I called out. I had never heard one before, and the sound was far off and indistinct, so I could not be sure. My friend Dennis Bires and I were facing east, the sun still 15 minutes below the horizon. On the Nature Conservancy's Tallgrass Prairie Preserve, at a pullout where the gravel road crests a ridgeline, we braced ourselves miserably against the wind. The predawn cold penetrated our clothes with

RICHARD HIGGS

stiff, bullying gusts that blew tears from our eyes. We cupped our hands to our ears and scanned left and right. It was during the month of April, or the Osage Planting Moon.

We were there to observe the crazy, predawn mating ritual of *Tympanuchus cupido*, commonly known as the greater prairie chicken, a rare sight, likely to become rarer still as their numbers and their habitat continue to dwindle. This preserve is one place where they've been able to make a stand.

Much of our misery was self-inflicted. The evening before, in camp, instead of prairie chickens in the grass, we'd found Wild Turkey in a flask. We'd sat facing the fire, as it settled into coals, and sipped our drinks until the fire was ready. Then, along with our dinner of oak-grilled venison, we'd polished off a bottle of cabernet. Dennis, big-game hunter, farmer, gourmand, and retired professor from the University of Tulsa College of Law, had provided food and drinks. After dinner, the flask had turned up empty. I'd lain down in my tent just before midnight.

The alarm startled me out of sleep and into a stupor at 4:30 a.m. I crawled out of my tent and stood reeling in the dark as Dennis emerged from his tent. It was a 40-minute drive to the viewing site, and we had to get there before sunrise.

It was imperative that I have coffee. Before I could make coffee, I had to build a fire. Before I could build a fire, I had to find a lighter. Dennis, always an organized camper, turned on his lantern, and everything flowed from that. Soon, we were well caffeinated and driving west.

Prairie chickens were once common throughout America's vast tallgrass prairies. Osage writer John Joseph Mathews used to drive his station wagon to a spot near a mating ground and watch their antics from close range, sitting in the back of his car. He wrote about them in his memoir *Talking to the Moon* in the 1940s:

> I have watched this dance every spring for years, and, as in the case of the Osage dances, I've never grown tired of it... Before the white man came to the Osage these grouse populated the range to the point of saturation and on April mornings filled the prairie with their booming as they danced on the high hills.

Searching for John Joseph Mathews

Despite the habitat pressures of intensive oil exploration in the area, Mathews was able to describe his pleasure in watching flocks of 30 to 40 as the hens gathered in a wide circle around the mating ground.

Inside the circle of hens, the cocks fan their tailfeathers, erect their pinnates, dance, leap, spar, lower their heads, inflate the saffron sacs on their necks and blowout their long, sonorous mating call. Peterson's *Field Guide to the Birds* describes the sound: " 'Booming' male in dance makes a hollow *oo-loo-woo*, suggesting the sound made by blowing across a bottle mouth." It can be heard over a mile away.

"I don't know, Rich. That could be a mourning dove," Dennis replied after hearing it again. We scanned the horizon in vain with our binoculars.

"Yeah. Probably a dove," I agreed.

The day had grown warm, sunny, and hypnotic by the time Dennis and I sat in the untended yard of Mathews' long-abandoned rock cabin, and quietly pondered his endangered legacy. We'd bounced gently along a serpentine, seldom-used lane for nearly a mile to reach the old house. The skeletal remains of a wisteria Mathews had planted were woven into the rusty wire fence around his yard. We could smell wild onions sprouting in the new spring grass. Through a screen of oaks, we looked down onto the surrounding sunlit prairie, which swayed in a wind that we could not feel.

Mathews rested in his grave across the yard in the shade of an old cedar tree. Behind us stood the little home he had ordered built, circa 1935, on his family's allotment, after several years of drifting through much of the Western world. He had lived alone there "in the blackjacks," as he called the place, for a decade. *Talking to the Moon* was his account of a typical year there. He divided the book according to the Osage moons. It was published in 1945. His widow, Elizabeth Mathews, begins her foreword to the 1981 edition: "This is John Joseph Mathews' *Walden*."

After his wanderings, Mathews returned home to Osage County because he'd had an epiphany, sometime in the late 1920s, while on a hunting trip in North Africa. He recalled the incident years later for Guy Logsdon in a conversation at the Osage Tribal Museum:

RICHARD HIGGS

I remember very distinctly one evening, when we were preparing our meal, suddenly it came to my guide and my cook that it was time to worship. So they fell on their knees, their faces toward Mecca, as usual. In this situation you feel so clumsy, so out of things—you feel that you are an absolutely sinful person. About this time some Kabyles, a wild tribe of Arabs, came up who were not Mohammedan and had no known religion at all—wild! They came racing across the sand. I think there were about six or eight of them firing their Winchesters, the model 1894 lever. I thought, here, we're in trouble. My guide and my cook were prostrate. They surrounded us shooting all the way on their Arab horses—all mares, incidentally. Then they got off and ate with us, they were very friendly. That night I got to thinking about it, and I thought that's exactly what happened to me one day when I was a little boy, riding on the Osage prairies. Osage warriors with only their breech-clouts and their guns had come up and surrounded me—firing. Of course, I knew some of them, about them; they knew me, who I was. That's what we called joy shooting, you see, just joy. So, I got homesick, and I thought, what am I doing over here? Why don't I go back and take some interest in my people? Why not go back to the Osage? They've got a culture. So, I came back; then I started talking with the old men.

Upon his return, Mathews devoted the rest of his life to chronicling the history and protecting the interests of the Osage Nation. He published five books, represented the tribe in Washington, D.C., facilitated the WPA-assigned oil portraits of Osage notables of the day, and was the driving force behind the creation of the Osage Tribal Museum, which recently celebrated its 75th anniversary.

At the time of his epiphany, Mathews was living in Switzerland, where he acquired a certificate in international relations from the University of Geneva, and attended the League of Nations sessions. He had come to Europe by way of Oxford University, where he'd earned a bachelor's degree in natural sciences from Merton College. Before Oxford, Mathews had acquired a degree in geology from the University of Oklahoma. As his time at OU came to an end, Mathews made a curious decision, detailed in Charles H. Red Corn's introduction to Mathews' autobiography, *Twenty Thousand Mornings*: "While waiting for graduation, he was approached about applying for a Rhodes Scholarship. After some soul searching, he proposed to... pay his own expenses, thus freeing up funding for someone not able to pay."As we strolled the grounds, musing over Mathews' reason for declining the scholarship, Dennis and I agreed that we'd rather believe he did it simply because the timing conflicted with his plans to hunt bears in Colorado, which is what he did, delaying his enrollment until after the hunt. Mathews had been to Europe before Oxford. During World War I, he interrupted his studies at OU to enlist in the armed forces. He served as a fighter pilot in the skies over France.

Mathews was born in Pawhuska, Oklahoma, on Agency Hill, November 16, 1894. In the introduction to *The Osages*, his history of the Osage Tribe, he tells this story from his Pawhuska childhood: "I was a very small boy when the seed which was to disturb me all of my life was planted." He'd been moved from his mother's bedroom because of the arrival of his baby sister, and given a room of his own. He'd lain awake all night, alone and afraid, as he recalls, "...I remember the hour before dawn, when the silence was the heaviest. There floated up to my room through the open window... a long, drawn out chant broken by weeping. It filled my little boy's soul with fear and bittersweetness..."

Looking back, he realized, "It was Neolithic man talking to God."

Mathews was an early environmentalist, but his motive for moving to the blackjacks was more personal than ideological. He wrote: "My coming back was dramatic in a way; a weight on the sensitive scales of nature, which I knew would eventually be adjusted if I lived as I had planned to live; to become a part of the balance." *Talking to the Moon* offers readers an example rather than a manifesto, which may be why his name, even in Oklahoma, is virtually unknown among environmentalists.

There is a photo from 1937 of Mathews sitting by his fireplace, pipe in hand. His hounds lay stretched out at his feet on a bearskin rug. Along the front of the fireplace mantle is this carefully hand-lettered Latin inscription: VENARI LAVARI LUDERE RIDERE OCCAST VIVERE, which

RICHARD HIGGS

Mathews had seen among some Roman ruins in North Africa; the motto of "some unit of the Third Augustan Legion" when that area was a Roman frontier in the first century. Mathews interprets it as TO HUNT, TO BATHE, TO PLAY, TO LAUGH—THAT IS TO LIVE." Dennis and I stood in the ruins of Mathews' cabin and pondered the still-readable inscription. Dennis, who knows his Latin, suggested an alternate translation:

"When Romans went to the baths," Dennis explained, "they were engaging in social recreation in what we today would describe as a swimming pool. So *lavari* could be loosely translated as 'to swim,' in much the sense Americans might use when they 'go out for a swim' in a back yard pool or an Osage County swimming hole. And an alternate translation for *ludere* is 'to make love.' It is entirely possible that Mathews, classically educated at OU and Oxford, translated the inscription for himself 'to hunt, to swim, to make love, to laugh—that is to live,' though he was perhaps too discreet to put it that way in writing."

Also in the photograph, on the mantle above the inscription, are two stuffed prairie chickens. The man loved to hunt.

Standing in Mathews' room surveying the collapsing roof, the fallen ceiling plaster, the glassless windows with rotted frames, I imagined the building and grounds restored to the conditions he'd kept, and made available, for short, spartan stays, to poets, writers, artists, and scientists whose works were relevant to the grass and trees outside. The walls, fieldstones 18-inches thick, are still strong and true. But a counter-thought intruded: Let the earth take it back, bit by bit, until even the stones have been pulled back below the soil, relieving the sensitive scales of their weight. Which would be the greater honor to Mathews' legacy?

If a snake were slithering along in definite search for food, and suddenly he became aware of the shadow cast by the wings of a red-tail hawk, high-circling, he would draw his head back and retract his body until it formed into a series of half-loops, then he would freeze, with only his forked tongue darting for messages. He would be like a carelessly dropped rope; like a new rope that had not the kinks stretched out of it.

That is the way the Osage River of central Missouri and eastern Kansas looks, as it comes down from the high prairie to flow through the wooded hills. It lies shining there, among the hills, like a snake under the shadow of wings, or like one that had been touched on the end of the nose by a snake stick.

—*The Osages: Children of the Middle Waters* by John Joseph Mathews, 1961

In the afternoon, we visited the Osage Tribal Museum. Uncombed, unshaven, wind burned, and reeking of camp smoke, I approached the gift counter and asked if they had any of Mathews' works for sale. I was referred to the public library. Although one cannot buy his books there, traces of Mathews are evident. There is a plaque with this inscription:

Devoted to preserving the culture and history of his Osage tribe and inspired by the natural world of the Osage Hills, the written works of John Joseph Mathews evoke the enduring spirit of the land and the people. Here on Osage Agency Hill, Mathews' birthplace, the Osage Tribal Museum, established in 1938 primarily through his efforts, is designated a Literary Landmark by the Association of Library Trustees, Advocates, Friends and Foundations. November 17, 2009. There are the WPA portraits that he facilitated; there is a formal portrait of him; there is his name among the original allottees; and, there is the museum itself.

Next morning at dawn, we parked where the gravel road veered north, but the fence line continued east. Meadowlarks sang out from all directions as we exited the pickup. We closed the doors quietly, and began to hike along the fence line, up the still-shaded slope of a rounded ridge. The previous day, in a chance encounter, we'd gotten a tip from Bonnie Gall, a volunteer at the Sutton Avian Research Center, that atop this ridge might be a good place to watch the prairie chickens dance their ancient dance. Our legs and lungs felt good to be climbing. The morning breeze was fresh on our faces. Finally on the ridge, in the first rays of the sun, we stopped to catch our breath.

RICHARD HIGGS

All was grass, in shadows and light. To our south, the soft folds of a valley dropped ever deeper as the slender watercourse in its bottom meandered eastward and down. Across the valley, a coyote went about its morning mouse hunt, following its nose with that curious coyote gait of quick, short steps. Overhead, wave after wave of cormorants, black and silent, flew straight north in large V-formations, returning from Belize.

We turned to the north and scanned the ridge with our binoculars.

"I think I see one!" I called out.

A SYMPHONY OF BEES

Broken by war, a disabled vet finds a home among hives

By *Mark Brown*

OUT OFF ASPEN AVENUE, deep in the tree streets of Broken Arrow, a very typical three-bedroom, single-family unit is going rogue. If I hadn't gotten lost and texted the occupant for directions, I'm not sure I'd have noticed the quirks: a 10-foot stand of cane obscuring the brick mailbox, a rick of firewood parked where a car should be, the rolled up carpet and padding on the walkway, the security fence piled in the front yard. But he gave himself away.

"Bro ... it's the house that looks like a disabled vet lives in it."

The closer you get to the door, the more clues: a waist-high galvanized tub for catching rainwater beneath a bedroom window, and four foil-wrapped potatoes roasting in a small solar oven just off the porch. Then the door opens and, however prepared you think you are, you aren't.

"Come on in," he says, holding the doorknob with one hand and a coffee mug with the other. A long, black ponytail falls down between his shoulder blades. His eyes radiate a rich, deep brown, like the grain on a gunstock. He's wearing cargo pants, a black T-shirt, and a camo cap with a Velcro patch that reads, "Embrace The Suck." The Suck is soldier-speak for the frontlines and all they entail.

MARK BROWN

Fifteen feet inside the house, the step drops down into the living room, over which a rough-hewn sign proclaims, "Man Cave." It's a cave, all right, but the joke is lost somewhere in the pile of houseplants, empty pill bottles, and government mail. Two hammocks tied to the rafters with ropes and carabiners provide the canopy. Two pit bulls: a brown brindle named Beau and a white one named Luke lean up from their pallet.

"They're my gatekeepers," says the man of the house.

The dogs are sweet-faced and docile, if not outright timid. They eat Eagle Pack Holistic Select Lamb Formula chow, cans of which sit in a cardboard case just inside the room, likely where they were dropped. Two Catchmaster glue boards sit next to them, awaiting deployment. The carpet has been pulled, exposing the concrete, exposing the habits.

"No matter how much you try to stay on top of it," says the man of the house, "you can't keep it clean. I am a man, I have two dogs, a goat, four chickens, and at times in this house I've had a boa constrictor, a Sumatran water monitor, a possum, two coyotes … I mean, carpet doesn't necessarily work out in this environment."

If a man's home is his castle, this is a domain of disequilibrium. Like the clutter in its rooms, its owner has been misplaced. His file:

Kenneth Elliott Ambrose Heyne (say it HI-nee), age 30. U.S. Army Sergeant E-5, retired, or in the long and withdrawn process of becoming so. Date of induction: 29 February 2000. Leap Day. Officially decommissioned: 15 October 2007. Seven years and two tours, Iraq and Afghanistan. For his work, he received an MSM, a Meritorious Service Medal. He's also, by the Army's definition, 100 percent P and T—permanently and totally disabled. He says it's from sustained sleep deprivation, stress, and bombs. The Army may or may not be saying, but they admit that the guy they signed into service is not the one they discharged. They send him disability because they can't expect him to get or hold a job, not now. He proves their point on a near-daily basis. Exhibit A: Three years ago, he brushed 24-hour paint stripper on some kitchen cabinets he meant to repaint. It's still there.

"The reality is," Elliott says, "I'm a disabled vet, bipolar as fuck, and I just hadn't gotten around to it yet."

What he will do, and does, most mornings is go to the kitchen, get his first of many cups of Topéca, and go sit in his backyard, where two dogs, three chickens, and a Pygmy goat commune with some 60,000 Italian honeybees, *Apis mellifera ligustica*, a breed with a reputation for gentleness. The chickens

A SYMPHONY OF BEES

are for eggs—he had four but one of them got egg bound and died from the rupture; he could tell by the smell things were bad—the goat for kicks, and the honeybees for, believe it or not, companionship.

"If I'm not messing with them," he says, "I can sit right next to the hives. Honey is secondary right now. It's all about keeping bees alive, and whatever pleasure that affords. One of my favorite things to do is go out there in the morning, have my coffee, sit down, and watch my bees wake up. I try not to wear black stuff on my head."

Bees will attack black, but it's mostly what's in his head that raises flags. Something's gone missing in the Broken Arrow hive of Elliott Heyne. Primarily, Elliott Heyne. The discharged Army sergeant who used to be a voracious reader with the patience for Melville. The neat freak who had a place for everything and everything in its place. The infectious smile and laugh personified who can't remember the last time he was around somebody in an intimate fashion. Because that guy is long gone.

"I went from a period in my life where I was in control," he says, "or at least I thought I was, and all my actions had to reflect a specific intent. I had to have the proper motivation outlined. These days, none of that even enters my head. I'm off in my own world 90 percent of the time."

The other 10 percent his presence is desired in other places, but the stress of deadlines—where he actually has to be somewhere at a given hour—can deter him. Among more physical ailments. "If I'm in pain, my neck or back's hurtin', or like today, when I'm passing a kidney stone, deadlines just aren't fun. I'll get there when I get there. Until then, I'm gonna be where I'm at."

That's likely here, under the maple trees of South Aspen, among his beehives, in his bubble, mostly out of the way, and quietly embracing The Suck.

The world over, bees are dying in mortal combat. The hive is in shock, and the enemy has overrun the perimeter. Make that enemies: hive beetles, roaches, wasps, for starters, and unseen invaders—varroa mites that latch onto a bee's exoskeleton and suck out her hemolymph, and myriad insecticides, like the new-wave systemics applied at seeding. Foraging bees ingest them and, rather than die on the vine, carry the poison back to the

MARK BROWN

hive. The more noticeable invaders, Elliott squashes under his thumb. So far, in his three hives, the thumb's been enough.

"No fungus, disease, nothing out of the ordinary," he says. "It's hard to say how strong they are. We'll find out pretty soon, won't we?"

He baits them by pouring feed syrup on their doorstep. The bees take honey for primary nourishment. The syrup is insurance. Their keeper gets paranoid that they might store the syrup, though, instead of the honey.

"They'll go back into their hive and do their little shaky dance[1] and that sugar water'll be gone." Five gallons before the sun goes down. The bees suck the syrup off of the cane tops that Elliott snips and places into 5-gallon buckets. This keeps the cane from seeding and taking over his cul-de-sac. And it allows the bees cling to the fronds to keep from drowning in the sugar water. It's no random symbiosis, to hear it explained.

"If you look at how things have been going in the world lately, with the temperatures doing what they are here in Oklahoma, the flowers are pretty much done by June or July. Their ability to obtain nectar through natural food sources is disrupted. To supplement their diet, to make sure I maintain good healthy hives throughout the winter, I supplement with sugar water."

One of Elliott's roles as a sergeant was the training of Afghan National Auxiliary Police forces. His Form 214 service record lists four "achievements": four assignments in establishing, facilitating, and executing training programs for local militia. None of which reads like the charge up San Juan Hill. But modern warfare doesn't work like that, says Elliott. Modern war is routine mismanagement, contractors soaking off the backs

---

1. In *The Dancing Bees: An Account of the Life and Senses of the Honey Bee*, legendary bee man Karl von Frisch documented his discovery of the "waggle dance," a movement among foraging bees to indicate to other hive members the direction and distance of nectar-bearing flowers. "What makes it so particularly striking and attractive is the way it infects the surrounding bees; those sitting next to the dancer start tripping after her, always trying to keep their outstretched feelers in close contact with the tip of her abdomen. They take part in each of her maneuverings so that the dancer herself, in her madly wheeling movements, appears to carry behind her a perpetual comet's tail of bees." The dance done, the dancer leads her frenzied charges out of the hive.

A SYMPHONY OF BEES

of soldiers, an Army culture of unnecessary stress, and other things that suck. The hive affords no room for such disturbances. Any bee acting this way would have his arms ripped off, his abdomen gutted and his striped ass booted from the colony. Because the colony lives and dies on a collective adherence to one principle, that of the common good.

Honeybees fly sorties in and out of home base in search of nectar, which will become honey, but not in his hands. With its proboscis it angles for the sweet spot of the flower between the sepal and petal, for the flower water, fills its sac then flies home full up. To become honey, nectar is thickened with a collective flapping of wings—the water evaporates and the nectar thickens—by honey processors, bees born to the task. Division of labor[2] is alive and well in a beehive. There are nurse bees to care for the queen. (One of their roles is the decontamination of returning workers.) Guard bees for keeping out undesirables. Cleaning squads. Heating and cooling teams. Comb builders. Honey, thus, is born, like all sorts of sweet things, on the backs of workers.

"You can join the Army thinking you're going to be in personnel, or water filtration, or fuel supply, and the next thing you know you're going to be operating an entry control point into one of your camps, and you're going to be checking for vehicle-bound IEDs without any of the real training that job requires.

"See ... when you're in the military, you can be ordered."

The only thing keeping Elliott's backyard his backyard are the privacy fences. That's because he believes that a healthy ecosystem is a diverse one, and the zip code be damned. The more complex, the better. Three maples toss their twigs to the ground below. The Bermuda is thick, green, and

---

2. Von Frisch warned of the tendencies to align busy bees with human work. "We have already mentioned in passing that there exists a strict division of labour among the workers of a bee colony: some of them tend the brood while others see to the cleanliness of the hive; others again build the combs, defend the hive, or collect either honey or pollen. One is tempted to draw a comparison between these conditions and those prevailing in human society; we feel compelled to think of a human community with its teachers and policemen, street-sweepers and carpenters, bakers and confectioners. But the analogy remains only superficial."

185

MARK BROWN

wild. Elliott leaves the mycelium—the ground-feeding fungus—that you would root out. A Lifetime compost tumbler stands in the middle of the yard, awaiting its next meal. On the back porch, birds have built a nest in the fixture of a security light.

In Elliott's world, it can be difficult to tell outside from in, like over the threshold to the backyard, where cracks in the living room foundation—visible because, remember, he's ripped up the carpet—blur with the encroaching stalks of grass and weed. The barnyard he keeps seems all the happier for it. Three hens, one goat, named Jules, three beehives—"I can have four in Broken Arrow," Elliott says—and two pit bulls, Luke and Beau. "I haven't named the hens. I don't think it's proper to name things you might end up ... dining on."

Jules, after the homicidal, jheri-curled Jules Winnfield of *Pulp Fiction* infamy. She's about knee-high, with eyes that shine ice-blue with black New Wave slits. She'll run between the porch and the hives, bouncing across the rooftops as if they were mountain crags. Theoretically, if she's jumping on the hives and agitating the bees enough, she could die. But she hasn't riled them yet.

"She can leap up to a windowsill," Elliott says. She'll jump over his head if he's bent down. A Pygmy wouldn't eat a lot, he thought, and wouldn't be large enough to knock over a hive. "It takes about 1,800 stings to kill a human. But she was cute, adorable, and for sale. I can be incredibly impulsive at times."

He calms such impulses by volunteering at Wild Heart Ranch Wildlife Rescue. There, holding a baby deer or feeding a skunk or charming a pair of baby barn owls, he's a man of calm and inner peace, a condition he struggles with among humans.

"Elliott's passion stems from his having been broken down completely as a human being," said Annette King Tucker, Wild Heart founder and director. "His determination to heal himself has allowed him to see the world from another perspective without all the pointless daily clutter that most people carry around."

However comfortable he is among bees, I'm still a novice. You have to resign yourself to getting stung, and the lack of a memory for this pain is what makes such resignation possible. Either way, we've now been standing in the same spot long enough to draw attention. Nervous bees will alert an enemy by orbiting and occasionally head-butting. "I'm in black," Elliott said, grabbing at his T-shirt. "We're gonna need to move." Bees suspicion black. He could be a bear with an appetite for comb, for all they know. He's taking morphine for his kidney stones and doesn't want to push it, the cocktail of opiate and venom. "Anyway, we're about to crack into 'em and we don't want 'em to be angry."

By nature they aren't. Happy, docile, working, active is how he describes his honeybees. Stinging you is hardly priority one. "We're hard-wired to be afraid of what we don't know, and the first emotion we feel is fear. But I've always thought bees were cool. When I'm working with them I feel at home, comfortable, a part of something. Listen ... It's a little symphony all by itself." Indeed, the pitch changes, the music intensifies, the nearer you get. Elliott reaches onto one of the hive boxes and lifts off a dead worker. "This guy's a fresh one. He's just from last night."

A colony of bees will lose a quarter of its population in a season, from causes natural and violent, known and mysterious. He pulls it in close to examine. When he squeezes its abdomen, bee venom shoots out in a stream onto my sweater. "Sorry, dude," he says, with not a little sincerity.

A hive is a mass of wax, glue, honey, brood, enemies, and bees. Like anything thriving and organic, it's kind of a mess. But the bees know their way around it by instinct.

Likewise, there is a logic to Elliott's living room that evades the eye at first glance. A lot of what you might call half-assed is actually fairly thought out. Where you might hang shelves, he's bolted black milk crates and stuffed them with everything from plant food to surgical gloves. Where you might set a CD rack he stores a Shop-Vac. Ivy grows not on the house but in it. The bucket of coal and ash next to the fireplace is what he uses to heat his bathroom every morning. Next to the fireplace are the bookshelves. Before the ringing in his head made it nearly impossible, Elliott read. His shelves hold a small but inviting selection: Chuck Palahniuk, Helena Blavatsky, Hunter S. Thompson, Alice Bailey, Herman Melville, Mark Bowden's *Guests of the Ayatollah*. In the middle of the room is a table and, on it, a scattered inventory that includes King butane, Avant gauze, Thai Sriracha hot sauce, many spent Walgreens pill bottles, vascular clamps, BernzOmatic blowtorch, cork from a magnum of Chimay Grande Reserve, 1,000 milligram DHA omega-3 fatty acid, 10 Plus Cortizone, 3-inch Lodge

MARK BROWN

cast-iron skillet, blue Sharpie, Gorilla superglue, much unopened mail, some opened, and a single synthetic flower, a camellia maybe. Rising up out of this mix, an Apple computer. About to fall off the table, a carton of red Thai curry with an inch of sauce in the bottom. Elliott prefers to eat out, but, "When you get a good swerve on, it's just easier to go to the fridge and pull out some Pad Ped."

Stuck to his fridge are several tasty looking recipes for juicing: Lemony Apple, Beety Beauty, Apple Green Grape. He juices because of benign prostatic hyperplasia, or BPA. Elliott carries around with him the usual disabled vet's set of acronyms—PTSD, TBI—jargon he drops as a matter of fact. To explain how he got there, how it all went awry, he makes a lattice of his hands, the fingers hatched to represent the brain's patchwork of synapses. Then he rotates his hands to relate how they became, through the pummel of war, disconnected.

Much has been written lately of CCD, or Colony Collapse Disorder, a complete disabling of the honeybee hive. A lot of it has been alarmist rhetoric designed for nightly news titillation, but Hannah Nordhaus, in *The Beekeeper's Lament*, provides a solid account of the concerns keeps face by following one John Miller, a fourth-generation Mormon beekeeper whose bees summer in Idaho before being trucked to California in winter to pollinate the almond crop. Nordhaus' chronicling of Miller's frustrated efforts to keep bees alive enumerates the hurdles (chemicals, predators—everything from mites to thieves—government policy, poverty, small-farm exodus) encountered by the alchemists in this ancient art.

"One of the very first things I noticed," said Greg Hannaford of CCD, "it occurred in the beginning almost exclusively with commercial beekeepers, versus hobby keepers. But that doesn't tell us a whole lot."

Hannaford is a longtime keeper and member of the Northeast Oklahoma Beekeepers Association. He notes that commercial keeps have their bees forever on the move, but admits that's nothing new, that bee transporting goes back to the era of the Model T and even train travel. That leaves him looking at chemicals.

"We do have a new class of pesticides out there (systemics) and they act differently on organisms than traditional pesticides. They don't necessarily

A Symphony of Bees

kill the organism, but they disrupt its behavior. As an application, they're as safe on bees as any other."

Which is what scares him. The government, Hannaford said, doesn't look at sub-lethal effects when determining agricultural policy. Unless bees fall dead from insecticides, the burden of proof remains with the beekeepers versus the chemical companies. Big farming and bees make odd bedfellows: Without bees, crops would lose valuable pollinators. Without chemicals, there'd be no big ag. We've made the bed, Hannaford said, and now we're lying in it.

"Our food culture was developed in the '50s. After World War II, agriculture and food consumption in the U.S. fundamentally changed. We went from an agricultural economy to an urban economy. To feed everybody, farms got bigger. And we got more consumer-oriented. That's why we have to have new car models every year. Advertisers learned they can shape our perceptions."

With cars, and with honey. "Commodity honeys—the Walmart, off-the-shelf stuff—is all remarkably similar. It all looks like what ad agencies have taught us honey should look like."

Every spring, when Greg Hannaford's hives grow from a solid 70 to a robust 400, Elliott goes out to a farmer's field in Jenks to lend a hand. The hives occupy a fenceline that runs for yards and yards. Out past Karma Street, down Aquarium Drive, out in the amber waves of the Arkansas River bottoms, the twin stacks of a PSO power station lend an industrial foreboding to an otherwise rural idyll.

A former contractor, Hannaford makes his money selling not honey but bees. Bees and whatever intrigue they bring.

"The bees are as much therapeutic to him as anything," Hannaford said. "He's very intelligent, but his mind is so scrambled that he can't function in a normal work environment. He can work with those bees all day long and it just calms his soul. And I get some really good help."

Last summer, re-queening Hannaford's hives, Elliott took several stings on his gloveless hands. They were stings from partially Africanized bees bought in Texas, then married to Hannaford's Italians. When the African honeybee, *Apis mellifera scutellata*, cross with European honeybees, the latter become so-called Africanized hybrids. They tend to be more

MARK BROWN

aggressive than the Euros—our summer heat gets them hot under the collar—but they're still way more interesting in pillaging a queen and hive than they are you and yours.

Anyway, a dozen of them stung Elliott on the hands and arms. But, he says, "It did not have the effect that you would anticipate."

When the stinging sensation faded, he noticed his energy levels were "a little amped." For being in the sun all day, he had not one inkling of a headache. His mood was peaking, even before he got home.

By the time he'd settled in and the venom had coursed through his body, he started noticing the stingers still in his arms. He felt a vibe behind the eyes and his lips went tingly. That's when he began to see bees, heard their buzzing, felt their presence in their venom.

He takes Flexeril and Motrin three times a day for the neck pain he manages from getting thrown onto the roof of a vehicle on Jalalabad Road in Nangarhar Province near the end of his deployment in Enduring Freedom.

But not that summer day he didn't.

Even a cursory knowledge of honeybee behavior will guide you through five poems Sylvia Plath wrote four months before she took her life. The five were written in one week—October 3–9, 1962—likely as the hive was winding down for the season.

Plath found something favorable in the suits and veils of the local beekeepers. She was also drawn to the hive itself and its infectious vibe— bees are said to happily hum in the key of C—that turned treacherous in her ear: "I am not a Caesar. I have simply ordered a box of maniacs." In "The Swarm," the bees become Napoleon's battered army, running for cover to find solace in Flanders' muddy fields. A hive swarms when its queen deems the colony too large or endangered in its current hive. Swarming is typically a spring thing. In "Wintering," the drones are dead and the workers hunker down for the long winter's nap.

Before it was over, Sylvia Plath stuffed wet towels under the doors of her Primrose Hill flat and leaned her head forever into a gas oven while her brood slept down the hall.

A SYMPHONY OF BEES

It's warm, not hot, and Elliott's bees are thriving. They hover around the hive opening where the keep has strewn thick sugar water for sustenance. Occasionally, one will dart over the privacy fence to forage, perhaps, somewhere in the vicinity, off into the smoky evening sunlight of a crackly November, Indian summer, that cascades over the 1970s rooftops of Aspen Avenue. When it's hot, the bees spread out and all cling to the hive and buzz their wings, drawing air from the bottom of the hive and pushing it out the top. The lids have holes for aeration. Some workers will fly off for water, which they use for evaporative cooling. But the relentless hundreds of June and July have receded.

Approaching the hive at this hour is what I think it must be like to enter a meteor shower without a gravitational field. I kneel down within a few feet of a box to study activity. A box is three sets of frames stacked atop each other, the top one covered with a peaked, copper roof. Elliott gets his hive bodies online from Brushy Mountain Bee Farm because, in his words, he wants the best. Out of the Brushy Mountain Estates emerge a steady stream of lovely bees. Two or three begin to orbit my head. One hits me in the back. I move off trying not to panic, wondering if that thing about bees smelling fear is real.

Back by the porch, Elliott is fanning the flames on a small smoker filled with tree bark. "Smoke sends a signal of imminent threat," he said, pumping the bellows. Consequently, a beekeeper becomes less of one. Before he put his bee suit on to go into the hives, Elliott looked pretty threatening. With his Manchurian facial hair and the black rag holding his hair back, he reminds me of a young Alain Jourgensen, Ministry frontman, before the heroin bit him. Suited up, he's a spaceman, all baby steps and pre-programmed movements.

He lifts the lid, and then a metal screen called a queen excluder, which keeps her and her stable of drones out of the honey supers. If she were to lay brood in the honeycomb, it would make for a messy harvest. Bees crawl in and out of the narrow spaces between frames. He smokes them and they scurry.

Seventeen of the United States claim the European honeybee as their official state insect, including Utah, which was called Deseret by the Mormons who landed there. Later, the Mormons acquiesced to the tribal Ute, hence Utah. In the Book of Mormon, "deseret" meant "honeybee" in

MARK BROWN

the language of the Jaredites, a tribe believed to have escaped to America during the construction of the Tower of Babel.

Up close, it's easy to see why humans laud the industry of bees. They accumulate their nectar, pollinate much of nature, tend their hive and support each other with great energy in their few months of life. "Socialism and communism are based theoretically on the concept of the hive," said Greg Hannaford. "Everybody working together for the good of the whole. The difference being that honeybees have no concept of self-interest. With humans, that's kind of an ebb and flow. We like to think we're community-minded but, when it comes down to it, we're all about self-interest. That's just the way we're made." As Elliott says, "It's hard to relate nature with the world of man."

This is Elliott's first year of harvest. He cut his first hive out of an apartment at 21st and Olive.[3] His therapist likes to get him into anything he can do solo,[4] though he helps Hannaford in the spring, when his hives number in the hundreds. "From what I can tell," Elliott says through his netting, "beekeepers are generally my kind of people."

---

3. Von Frisch: "A colony of bees will sometimes escape from the beekeeper and settle in a wood in the hollow trunk of a dead tree. This is the original dwelling of the honey-bees; and as there were then many more hollow trees than in our own days of improved forest cultivation, no housing problem existed for bees in ancient times." When the colony gets too big to feed itself, the hive will swarm. Half of it will follow the queen to a new home elsewhere. The other half will remain and re-queen the hive. Swarming bees, until they find a home, are likely to ball up anywhere. One last June, in New York City, congregated on a side-view mirror of a Volvo station wagon.

4. There is precedent for this. "Beekeepers are not, typically, 'people people,'" writes Hannah Nordhaus in *The Beekeeper's Lament*. "They like to be outside, working with their hands, alone. After World War I, the U.S. and British governments promoted beekeeping as a career for disfigured or shell-shocked veterans because they could work on their own. A bee yard is a good place to hide from other people, and for that reason beekeepers are often secluded souls. This is ironic, because the creatures that they tend are so existentially social. Bees live and die in communities. 'Honeybees can flourish only when associated in large numbers, as in a colony,' Lorenzo Langstroth wrote. 'In a solitary state, a single bee is almost as helpless as a new-born child, being paralyzed by the chill of a cool Summer night.'"

A scraggly shoot from a nearby tree dangles over the hive and he hacks it off with a Gurkha knife. The same knife he saw an Afghani butcher a goat with in short order. He'll use the blade to pry open hive frames stuck together with propolis, a sticky resin of sap and other botanicals that bees use to shore up spaces in the comb. He'd use his hive tool if he could find it. "Bee glue," he says, poking at the golden-brown goop. "A month to themselves and they'll glue a box tight."

He pauses to poke into a spun web of silk and a spider fritters out: "Look at that, he's sacking my bees." He flicks it away and pulls the frame up by its edges. A mass of bees navigates its way around each other and over the surface of the comb. He looks for and fairly quickly spots the queen—her body is long, like a worker with a worm attached to it—then another predator. "A freakin' hive beetle ... that really twists my titties."

A single frame of comb will hold about 10 pounds of honey. A super will weigh 100 pounds, with honey and hive. He lifts and replaces them at an even pace, and not without grace, taking care not to crush anybody.[5] "That's another cool thing about bees. They're all girls." Most, anyway. The drones—the bees who would be king—exist for the sole purpose of impregnating the queen. But if they're not already dead (we didn't spot any) they soon will be. He leans in face first and breathes into the hive. "Carbon dioxide really flips their switches."

Elliott shot a video on his iPhone late last May, when the Jenks hives were hopping. He zoomed in with his camera, onto a pile of bees whose activity, if you could slow down and study it, would alarm you in

---

5. Rev. Lorenzo Lorraine Langstroth received a patent in 1852 for a moveable-frame hive. His design is essentially the hive in use today. "Langstroth was a minister with some emotional problems, and the bees helped calm his mind," said Greg Hannaford. "He focused extensively on bees, and a lot of his discoveries weren't original, but he did manage to state them in a practical way." Prior to Langstroth, harvesting honey was deadly work, and not on keepers. Von Frisch certainly found comfort in it: "Thus, whenever there is anything to examine or to repair inside the hive, each comb can be lifted out separately with its frame and then put back again. Also it is possible to remove each separate framed comb when filled with honey, and to replace it with an empty frame without unduly disturbing the colony. With the old types of hive, extraction of honey meant destruction of the dwelling, and more often than not, annihilation of the whole colony."

MARK BROWN

its precision. Mostly what you see is a mass of busy bodies. It's what you hear that haunts.

"They say static is the leftover radiation from the Big Bang," Elliott says into the mic. "There's something about this sound that reminds me of that. Nature, and the laws of nature. The hum, the buzz, the frequency ...

"This is almost like a religious experience out here, and I am not the religious type."

About halfway in he turns the camera on himself and begins to rhapsodize. Among beekeepers, even ones in bee suits and veils, this is not an uncommon occurrence.

"When you're around a lot of this buzzing like this," Elliott says, "usually the bees are testy and territorial. It can be intimidating. But it keeps me calm."

Not to say they don't go nuts, he says. Sometimes, when he lifts the lid off a hive, the bees will dive-bomb his veil, aiming at the face behind it. The bee bombing is more tranquil, he maintains, than the roar of fighter jets overhead. In mid-sermon, a single bee lights on his shoulder and pauses for the camera.

"I *so* dig this. Can you hear that?"

He wishes you could hear the wings that buzz his ears. There's a pattern, he says—a symmetry to the sound—but still an element of chaos.

"To be home, and comfortable, and a part of something." He preaches it through the veil, a pair of sunglasses hiding the light of his eyes, searching for the words that must stand in for the sound that is all around. On the ground, in the air, piled onto the side of the box in what looks like a bee orgy until you look closer.

"Can you hear that?" he asks again.

It's like wind, until one of them whips by his mic, then it's like fire. He smokes them, they scurry. He sets down the smoker, picks up the iPhone, and then...

"Can you *hear* that? Is *that* a little different!"

The bees are in orbit, an interstellar hoedown promenading around the moon that is Elliott Heyne. A lone white tuft of cloud floats on a blue sky. The bees are going ape shit, as the keeper might say, a smile lighting up his face. Bees are raining horizontally, driving diagonally, skating out aerial figure eights, punching the silence with their winged symphony.

A Symphony of Bees

The sound, the sound … it's something you want to swat at in a past life, until you learn what the bees are up to, until you know.

He yells in that guttural U.S. Army way of his: "Idn't that the fuckin' *tits*, man!"

A STILLER GROUND

A father's meditation on the loss of his daughter

BY *Gordon Grice*

1

I WALKED IN GRAVEYARDS, gathering trash and fallen branches. I pulled weeds that obscured the names on old headstones, and, when I was through, most of the names I'd revealed meant nothing to me. I took special care with the graves of children. I put the ceramic animal caricatures back on the stones they'd fallen off of. After a rain, I thumbed mud from the Lucite-covered photographs set in stones. I took the time to read a turn-of-the-century marker made of crudely hand-lettered cement. On it was an asymmetric heart pieced from small stones. I subtracted compulsively; death year minus birth year equals age, give or take one.

I started, almost always, with the graves of my own ancestors and cousins. My mother's mother, dead before I was born. Carved next to her name was my grandfather's. He was still alive, though his name had been written in the city of the dead for 34 years. My cousin, a suicide at 21. His epitaph declared his heart too big to last in this world. I read his stone with double vision: the disdain I'd always had for such sentiments; the tolerance I had now for anything, anything at all, to ease the pain. I walked along the rows, taking care of people past caring.

GORDON GRICE

That was my daily routine. Sometimes the woman I loved would come with me. I envied her. She seemed to know how to grieve. To let herself feel things, to take time. She wrote letters to our stillborn daughter. She ordered photographs from the hospital and put them in a scrapbook. She talked. Most of these activities were strange to me, though I clumsily tried to emulate her for the sake of my mental health. I wanted to have my private scene at the cemetery, unwitnessed, and be cured for good, or at least for a little while.

Usually the last grave we visited was Abby's, on the western edge of the cemetery, a new section where shade trees were forbidden and the buffalo grass grew sparse. Around the temporary steel marker clustered a miniature rose bush and a petunia, both recently planted and probably doomed by the heat, and an assortment of artificial flowers. I rinsed the fake flowers every day. Despite my care, mud splashed them and became a coat of dust by the following day. Their brilliance evaporated. My mind crawled sluggishly into the groove of trite symbols—life is transitory as a spring rose, and that sort of thing. I despised such easy comparisons even as I dredged them from my stock of clichés.

One day the petunia bore the marks of some small nibbling animal. The next day the entire plant had been devoured, and rabbit scat lay among the artificial flowers. I cleaned things up. A black string lay on the ground, and as I knelt closer the string resolved itself into a trail of ants. They came out of a small hole in the ground, traveled a few inches, and vanished into another hole.

The ants reminded me of a long dream I'd had the night before. It ended with bullies throwing black ants on my daughter. She looked about four years old. I couldn't protect her. I was a bad father. The dream had clung for hours, souring the morning.

Now I knew what it meant. Ants eat dead things.

2

At the hospital the day Abby was born, a nurse handed me a booklet about being the parent of a dead child. What's the cost of a funeral for a newborn? Can you take a tax deduction? What should you name a dead child? Is it OK to build the coffin yourself? The booklet plainly answered

A Stiller Ground

such questions. It was my introduction to a realm of knowledge I had never known existed.

The answers run like this:

You can build the coffin if you want. It might make you feel better.

Name the child what you meant to name him. Don't save the name for someone else.

You can claim the baby as a dependent on your taxes if he drew a breath.

General practice in the funeral industry is to charge low for a baby. In Guymon we had two mortuaries to choose from, and I chose the one that had buried my grandmother. The man at the funeral home appeared well-muscled and athletic, out of place in his gray suit. He sold me a baby-sized Styrofoam coffin not unlike a picnic cooler. I paid $250 for it, and that was all I paid for the whole job. The athletic man asked me if anyone would view the body, and I said no. He asked me if I was sure, and I said I was. I thought it was a strange thing to ask. No one would want to look at a stillborn child. The last look is for someone you've seen before, and no one had seen Abby except Tracy and me and some strangers.

When Tracy's grandmother asked if she could see the body, I felt overwhelmed with gratitude. Abby was a real person, and now someone besides Tracy and me was saying so, however indirectly. Others had given us words of comfort that cut to the bone: *When this happens, it means something was really wrong with them. It's for the best. You'll have others. At least it happened before you got to know her.* All of which seemed to say Abby was not worthy of the grief.

I called the athlete to ask if it was too late to look at Abby, and it was.

"I'll tell you what," he said. "The casket's glued shut, but I can try to pry it open." That seemed a violation of the dead. I declined his offer. Later, when I saw the ants at the grave, I remembered the sealed Styrofoam. Maybe the ants weren't getting in. But something was happening to her, by whatever physical agent. Her decomposition was inexorable.

3

We were living in Arkansas, where we were in grad school, when Tracy got pregnant. It was a long drive from our hometown in the

GORDON GRICE

Oklahoma Panhandle. We had planned the pregnancy, and in October it happened. Not long after conception, Tracy bled, and we feared we'd lose the baby. Tracy had to stay in bed a while. Then everything smoothed out. In December I landed a teaching job back home in Oklahoma. The higher pay meant Tracy could stay home with the baby. We moved to Oklahoma in January.

Near the end of April, the pregnancy was 30 weeks along. Tracy hadn't felt the baby kick for a day or two, which worried me. I dismissed that fear, as I had many others over the months.

Tracy couldn't dismiss it, though she wasn't ready to press me with her worry. She remembered feeling the baby kick the previous Saturday, several fast kicks. She put her sister's hand on the place to let her feel, but there was no more movement. Later Tracy would wonder if those movements were caused by fear or pain. She would be haunted by the thought that those kicks marked the moment of death.

On Tuesday morning, Tracy was asleep when I left for work. When she woke, she tried to remind herself that babies sometimes don't move for long periods late in a pregnancy. Her sister Corey told her our nephew Cody had laid still in the womb for two days just before he was born. Tracy's stomach felt different, softer, and she tried to explain that away. And down deep, she knew the baby was dead.

Corey and Cody went with her to the doctor's office, where an experienced nurse failed to find a heartbeat. The nurse, an old family friend, didn't state the obvious conclusion. Tracy didn't say the words either. The nurse sent her to the hospital, where she waited with Corey and 14-month-old Cody.

Tracy held Cody and sang to him. She sang "Me and Bobby McGee," a song she'd sung to him many times before. She always meant for her own baby to hear it too. Somewhere she'd read that babies are soothed by songs they first learned in the womb. After an hour's wait, the hospital technicians were ready for her. She submitted to an array of machines—fetal monitor, X-ray, sonogram. The technicians said nothing about the baby. Each technician did his work, patted her on the arm, and left the room without a word.

When I got home from work, no one was there. I had a snack and turned on the TV. Then I saw a blinking light on the answering machine, and somehow I knew everything. The telephone rang. It was Corey. She

A STILLER GROUND

told me to come to the hospital. Before I left, I listened to the message on the answering machine, and of course it only said the same thing my sister-in-law had just told me.

At the hospital I found Tracy getting a sonogram. The room was dim, its fluorescent lights shaded by wooden blinds, the monitor casting a green light. The technician moved the probe soundlessly across Tracy's body, making furrows in the green lubricating jelly. The look on Tracy's face when she saw me was almost an apology: Surely this is nothing and it's a shame you had to worry about it, I hope. Corey yielded her position at the bedside and slipped out. The green shapes on the monitor moved with the motion of the technician's hand, forming pictures like those the weather people show on TV, storms forming, detected by shifting velocities, painted in thicknesses of a single shade. I couldn't see any image in the shifting green. The technician said nothing.

We went to a waiting room, where Tracy's family had gathered. It was a long wait. We saw the doctor arrive. He walked past the door of the waiting room to the sonogram room, and a minute later he was with us.

"It doesn't look good," he said. He hardly paused after that sentence, but for both of us the little pause was filled with frantic silent interpretation. He continued: "We've lost the baby."

4

"Here we see a double outline of the skull, and this is another indication of fetal loss," said the obstetrician we'd driven 40 miles to see. Our family doctor had sent us. The obstetrician traced the double outline with the blunt end of a pen on the sonogram screen.

"Is it a girl?" Tracy said.

"I don't see any indication of a boy," the obstetrician said.

It was Wednesday, the day after we found out. Everything was confirmed. He outlined the options: Wait for the baby to come to term, which could be two more months. A hard two months to go through, he said. Or take the baby out by cesarean. Hard on the mother's body; and you're robbed of everything about your baby, even the birth itself. Or induce labor. We chose the last. There was a rustling of papers as a nurse came in and out, offering us choices for an appointment at the hospital.

GORDON GRICE

The obstetrician inserted some sticks made of seaweed into Tracy's cervix. The idea was that they would absorb moisture overnight, expanding, dilating the cervix. Then, early in the morning, they'd give Tracy a drug to start contractions.

5

At the hospital the next day, a nurse took the booklet from me and turned to a certain page and pointed. "This is a list of what some people like to keep. If you two will circle what you want, I'll see you get it. Also, if you'll look at this other list and tell me what you want to do with the baby. I'll check with you later."

The baby was not yet born. Tracy lay in a hospital bed, clutching a sort of joystick with a button that coaxed morphine through an IV drip. A machine with red liquid digits rationed out the drug, keeping her from getting too much.

The suggested keepsakes included a lock of hair, inked footprints and handprints, a birth certificate, the plastic hospital bracelet, the receiving blanket, various bits of paperwork. And photographs.

I didn't want the photographs. The very thought of having such a thing repulsed me. A dead baby. You wouldn't want it, I reasoned—it seemed like reasoning—because someone else might come across it, might without preparation or desire see a dead baby. Where would you keep such a picture?

"In a photo album," Tracy said. She lay on her side, her hair clinging to the sweat of her neck, occasionally whimpering with pain—something I'd never heard her do. She lay there with her fist wrapped around the morphine button, her eyes almost closed against the pain, and knew exactly what she would want later. I stood there feeling embarrassed at the thought of photographs of the dead, but my embarrassment, I would decide later, was really shame. The shame of a failed father.

I massaged Tracy's back, because they'd said in childbirth class that relaxing was supposed to lessen pain, and because I had nothing else to do.

6

Eight hours after the IV drip started to convulse her body, Tracy said she had to urinate. The nurse asked her how long it had been and threatened to run a catheter. As she sat up, Tracy said, "Oh!" She pushed away the nurse who was still trying to help her stand. "I think my water broke."

Minutes later the obstetrician was back, and other nurses, and the pushing started. Tracy screamed. After the hours of helpless inertia, she was sitting up, straining her muscles, her eyes wide and bright.

"Don't scream, honey," the head nurse said.

Tracy thought she had to be kidding. "It seemed like a stupid thing to say," she told me later. "I thought I should get to scream if I wanted to." She screamed again, and her whole body seemed to strain into that primal sound. It seemed closer to anger than pain.

"Don't scream, honey," the head nurse insisted quietly. "Use that strength to push."

"Really?" Tracy said, as if someone had just dropped an interesting fact in casual conversation. She didn't scream again.

I stood holding Tracy's hand, and I cried as I never had before. The day had seemed long and tense and irritating, and now all the tense irritation unmasked itself as grief and overwhelmed me with tears. I was trying to help. Nothing we'd learned in childbirth class, nothing I'd read in the books held any relevance here. The head nurse told Tracy what to do, speaking in a compassionate whisper that Tracy could hear in spite of my blubbering. I was supposed to let Tracy squeeze my hand when she needed to. With the other hand I continually wiped my eyes so I could see what was going on.

Beneath the foot of the bed lay a pool of blood, shimmering in the fluorescent light. Most of it had fallen there when the water broke, but there was still a steady drip from the bed. I marveled at the sloppiness of it. You'd think they'd have a way to keep it from getting in the works of the bed and all, I thought. The obstetrician sat on a swivel stool, crouched like a watchmaker going about some routine task at the work bench. He stuck his finger in to stretch the opening. It seemed to me he had nothing better to do. The baby's head appeared, dark curls plastered to bright red skin, pushing through a little wave of slimy fluid.

GORDON GRICE

"It's crowning," the doctor said. What a useless son of a bitch you are, I thought.

"Jesus, that hurts," Tracy said, without any particular intensity. The baby came out surprisingly fast, falling audibly on the padded shelf the doctor had pulled out of the bed. Her entire body was bright red, as if she were blushing deeply, and covered with the waxy white substance called vernix. Otherwise, she looked like any other baby. The cord trailed out with her, fleshy and also blushing. It was tied in a red knot.

"That might explain something," the doctor remarked mildly.

"There's a knot in the cord," I sobbed.

"Oh," Tracy said.

"Could that have killed her?" I said.

"Yes," the doctor said. "It could have." He poked at the knot with some surgical instrument. "Not very tight, really."

Shut up, you useless son of a bitch, I thought. This is an explanation. Don't ruin it.

7

Tracy's mother was in the room, but she didn't want to see Abby. She looked at Tracy's face throughout the labor, and never saw the body. When a nurse mentioned holding Abby, Tracy's mother left the room.

The booklet the nurse had given me suggested things to do. Hold the body; bathe it; rock it; take pictures; dress it; talk to it; invite the family in to see it. Touching was supposed to make it easier to heal because you have to have a tactile sense of somebody to remember. All of these struck me as weird and disturbing at first mention. But the book said I'd be sorry if I never held her, and that sounded plausible.

A nurse took Abby out to clean her up a bit. Shortly she was back, carrying Abby in a white receiving blanket with a few stripes on it. She made a ridiculously small bundle, which the nurse handed to Tracy.

"She's beautiful," Tracy said, pulling the blanket away from her face to see her better. We made inventory. One foot was cramped into an odd position, and the nurse said that would have straightened out in a little while. Tracy claimed her ears looked like mine.

I was still crying and not saying too much. "Can we open the eyes?" I finally choked out.

"No, it's better if we don't," said the nurse with the hushed but strangely audible voice. I wanted to know what color her eyes were, and I didn't know a newborn's eyes may not settle on a color for several months.

When it was my turn I sat and rocked Abby. An errant smudge of blood stained my shirt cuff. It was not really Abby's blood, but placental blood. Still, I thought of it as hers. I'd been meaning to return the shirt because of its shoddy workmanship, but now I realized I never would. A corner of her right eye had worked itself open, and the crescent of color I saw was dark.

8

That night I lay beside Tracy's bed in a reclining chair. I wrapped myself in a sheet and a thin blanket and lay there sweaty and cold, my neck crimping. I slept a little. What kept waking me was baby-sound. The nursery was nearby. The cries would come, thin as wet slivers of rosewood, and I would wake. They sounded less than real, like cries on TV do. I liked to hear them.

Glass vases with thin necks lined the windowsill. A rank of white irises traced cloud-shapes against the dark of the real clouds behind them. The moon was bright. I fell in and out of dreams. In one dream the doctor suddenly realized we had two children, and he took Tracy into surgery to cut out the unborn twin. It was a boy, monstrously large, and instead of his sister's fatal softness he had a hard skull and great predatory teeth. But he cried, helpless as a human child. His eyes were wild, ape's eyes, nothing human in them except the need to be fed, and Tracy and I would have an unrelenting lifetime of hunger and screams.

When I woke I was not scared, only lonely. I lay awake listening to Tracy's breathing and the cries of the distant children.

9

It was 40 miles from hospital to home. Tracy sat quietly. After the long labor with its violent artificial contractions, they'd taken her into surgery to scrape out the recalcitrant placenta. She was in considerable pain.

GORDON GRICE

A snowstorm had blown up that morning. Its gusts danced on the highway like white dresses on a wash line. On the car stereo, which had been a birthday present to me the week before, we had Billie Holiday, and she was singing "Summertime." In the song a mother is singing to her baby. She says the living is easy. She says one day the baby will rise up singing and spread his wings and take to the sky, but till then he's safe with his father and mother.

When we got home I took two days' worth of mail from the box. All of it was damp along the edge where snow had blown in. There were bills and business and letters from friends, as if nothing had happened.

10

I didn't sit and brood about Abby all the time. I thought of her often, many times in a day. Sometimes I thought of her with nothing but pleasure. Tracy and I both found the memory of her birth profoundly beautiful, despite everything. But the grief returned frequently. It would start as an irritable feeling, hardly noticeable to me, though no doubt others found me harder than usual to get along with. Over the course of a week or so, my irritability would blossom into a restless insomnia and an unfocused anger. Eventually I'd find myself up long past midnight, pawing through the months-old sympathy cards and the toys people had sent in anticipation and the photos and the birth certificate and the footprints and handprints.

I was happy if I could draw tears. Tears would make me feel sane for a few days or a few weeks. But everything would start over, the grief cycling in unpredictable intervals. Sometimes it came as a sudden catch in my voice, or as a craving for hard-driving rock and roll, or as a suspicion that I had somehow killed her. Sometimes it came as a diffuse hunger that seemed to have no object, an almost subliminal feeling that I could satisfy myself with a meal or a drink or a sudden insight.

Sometimes it was a daydream. In one of them I found myself holding her in some realm outside of time, and I was telling her everything would be all right.

11

My mother admitted she was mad at God. She would go to the grave and sing lullabies and check on the flowers. If the flowers faded, she'd ask Tracy's permission before she took them up. Before she left the cemetery she always traced the name on the iron marker with her finger.

One day, not long after Oklahoma's fitful spring returned, Tracy and my mother went to the cemetery together. They found the deep gouge of a tire across the grave. The tire had bent the iron marker. Tracy had a habit of putting a pretty rock on the grave every time she visited. The rocks were scattered, and one of them, a rough cluster of quartz crystals, had broken. It lay scattered on the road like rock salt.

The tire track guided them to another grave nearby, freshly dug, heaped up with wet clods of earth the color of unripe peaches. Some workers had run over the older grave on the way to digging the new.

"It felt like they had hurt her," Tracy told me later.

The two women took up the trash of ruined flowers and salvaged what they could. They raked the grave level. They even wrestled the marker back into shape.

When they told me what had happened, I went to look for myself. Then I went home and started making phone calls. A man in charge of the cemetery agreed to meet me there.

"This is my daughter's grave," I said. When he saw the tracks he apologized repeatedly. He shook my hand in an unchallenging grip and said he would personally see that everything was put right. He gave me his personal phone number and assured me he would instantly resolve any problem for me, though, he hastened to add, he would see to it that no other problem ever arose.

I said, "All right," and drove home. I was angry because the man had given me no chance to start a fight. When I got home I took a handsaw up a tree and worked at a branch, my strokes frantic and ineffectual, the saw continually jumping out of its groove to start a new cut. Soon I was tired and sweaty. The bark was scored in a dozen places, but the heartwood remained unscathed. I climbed down and sat on the porch drinking iced tea. Tracy joined me.

"Caring for a grave is a lousy substitute," she said.

GORDON GRICE

12

Someone told me my dead grandmother would watch over her in heaven. I took comfort in that, even though heaven struck me as implausible. I pictured my grandmother in the dress they buried her in, which she'd never worn in life. I pictured Abby on her lap. But I couldn't see Abby's face, because I had forgotten it.

I got out the photos the hospital had sent us, the disturbing Polaroids with the blood-red lips and the better ones with her the way I remembered, or would have remembered if everything weren't slipping away from me. You don't remember her face, I told myself. Now you remember the photos of her face. You held her for half an hour; you've held the photos longer than that. I found I had an idea of her personality, which I based on nothing but the face in the photos. She was a serious little girl, given to wrinkling her brow irritably at the silliness of others. The sort of person who listens closely when you speak and then asks blunt questions.

13

One morning in April I lay in bed hoping the phone wouldn't ring. I needed work, but hoped nobody would call to give me any that day. It was two days until my birthday, and after that it would be one more week to Abby's birthday: one year old.

The day was misty and cold. I warmed some vegetable soup and sat on the couch in front of the TV. When the picture came on I saw an aerial shot of a building from which a section seemed to have been bitten. After a while I gathered that the building was in the capital city of my own state, and that people were dead and others bloody on the street. The dead were numerous, and many of them children.

In the ensuing weeks, one of those children came to stand for all of them in the newspapers and magazines. She was one year old. An often-printed image showed her, newly dead, in the arms of a fireman. A single idea came to dominate captions of her image: the heroism of the rescuers.

That's not what it means, I thought. That's not it at all.

A STILLER GROUND

14

To the east, where most of the graves lay, were a few stands of pine. One day, in a pause between rains, I watched a flight of birds wheel above gray puddles, and reflected in the puddles were multiples of the sky: the jagged line of pines, the stacked clouds solid as cut limestone, the dark birds arcing. The birds made tight turns—how did they synchronize?—and suddenly were absorbed in the still trees. It took my eyes a moment to pick out the individual birds standing silent in the boughs.

As our car crept along the narrow lanes of the cemetery toward the exit, Tracy and I discussed the birds. They seemed to always be there. I thought they were crows. I had once seen crows picking through the rubble of a car wreck, the windshield broken into blood-smeared gravel and gleaming under their delicate iron feet. I'd seen them at the carcasses of mule deer and coyote on the highway. They should roost in a cemetery, I thought. It would be a nice symbol.

Tracy thought they were grackles. "They're smaller than crows," she said. "And look how their heads are midnight blue instead of black."

I will never forget her, I found myself thinking. I will never forget, I will never forget. But I will, won't I? When I die.

That thought had been hurting me like a fresh bruise all day. When Tracy and I are dead, no one will remember that a girl named Abby ever was. I thought of my youth slipping away from me, of the fact that I too would one day be buried in a cemetery—maybe this one—among the ants and the murder of birds in the pines. It was the old but always fresh insight that the death of the child is also the death of the parent, and that nothing taken by the ants can ever come back.

"These never seem to make any noise," I said aloud. "If they said something, you could tell whether they're crows."

Just then one of the birds came up from the ground, flapping at an indolent pace. It seemed as if it should crash, but instead it cruised at four feet, crossing in front of our windshield. Grasped in its blue-black feet, complete, as yet unmutilated, almost surreal in the crisp perfection of its details, was a cottontail rabbit kit. The bird curved its flight to the ground in front of a red-granite headstone.

"Drive on," Tracy said. "Fast." She was pregnant again, and easily made sick.

15

The spring warmed up, and every night on the news they numbered the dead from the Murrah Building in Oklahoma City. Friends and relatives who'd been in the city on business recounted their stories, except for one man who'd helped dig out the children. He kept silent about it.

One night the news was interrupted every few minutes with tornado warnings. I didn't much care. We had a lot of tornado warnings in Oklahoma, and who has time to run for shelter with every warning? Outside the air was muggy and gray and smelled as if it might break into lightning. I had a backache. Not the kind that really hurts, just the kind that tells you there's weather out. I walked in the yard, watching a scatter of ants scramble against the coming of the rain. What were they in such a hurry to do? Probably they meant to seal themselves in against the storm. So why were they all outside their den?

I had recently read about the Torajan people of Indonesia. They inter dead children in cavities hewn in trees. The tree slowly closes its wound around the child. The tree keeps growing in the child's place.

I watched the clouds and the ground by turns. The storm stacked up. The ants vanished, as if absorbed into the dry ground about to take the rain.

INDEX

BY AUTHOR

Ball, Natasha
    Introduction **v**
    Home on the Range **67**

Barbery, Marcos
    From One Fire **1**

Brown, Mark
    A Symphony of Bees **181**

Cates, Hunter Howe
    Youngwolfe Accused **35**

Chapman, Lee Roy
    Subterranean Psychonaut **115**

Christian, Jason
    Terror's Legacy **51**

Cobb, Russell
    Locker Room Confidential **73**

Gerkin, Steve
    Watts and Clary **43**

Gillium, Mitch
    Weird Al-Chemy **153**

Grice, Gordon
    A Stiller Ground **197**

Higgs, Richard
    Searching for John Joseph
    Mathews **171**

Jones, Brian Ted
    Dogs Playing Poker **59**

Lloyd, Jennie
    Horses and Dagger **81**

Mason, Michael
    Subterranean Psychonaut **115**

McGirk, James
    Petro State **105**

Sandel, Chris
    Subterranean Psychonaut **115**

Sherman, Steve
    Pop Life **159**

Stone, Cortney
    Borrowed Notes **165**

Wall, Holly
    Snakes on a Plain **95**

BY ISSUE NUMBER

ISSUE 2, JANUARY 15, 2013
A Symphony of Bees
by Mark Brown **181**

ISSUE 4, FEBRUARY 15, 2013
Home on the Range
by Natasha Ball **67**

ISSUE 8, APRIL 15, 2013
Horses and Dagger
by Jenny Lloyd **81**

ISSUE 10, MAY 15, 2013
From One Fire
by Marcos Barbery **1**

ISSUE 11, JUNE 1, 2013
Dogs Playing Poker
by Brian Ted Jones **59**

ISSUE 13, JULY 1, 2013
Youngwolfe Accused
by Hunter Howe Cates **35**

ISSUE 14, JULY 15, 2013
Subterranean Psychonaut
*by Michael Mason,
Chris Sandel, and Lee
Roy Chapman* **115**

ISSUE 15, AUGUST 1, 2013
Terror's Legacy
by Jason Christian **51**

ISSUE 16, AUGUST 15, 2013
Searching for John Joseph
Mathews
by Richard Higgs **171**
Watts and Clary
by Steve Gerkin **43**

ISSUE 17, SEPTEMBER 1, 2013
Snakes on a Plain
by Holly Wall **95**

ISSUE 18, SEPTEMBER 15, 2013
Pop Life
by Steve Sherman **159**

ISSUE 19, OCTOBER 1, 2013
Borrowed Notes
by Cortney Stone **165**

ISSUE 20, OCTOBER 15, 2013
Weird Al-Chemy
by Mitch Gilliam **153**

ISSUE 22, NOVEMBER 15, 2013
A Stiller Ground
by Gordon Grice **197**

ISSUE 23, DECEMBER 1, 2013
Locker Room Confidential
by Russell Cobb **73**
Petro State
by James McGirk **105**

CPSIA information can be obtained
at www.ICGtesting.com
Printed in the USA
BVHW081014030919
557416BV00002B/238/P